SpringerBriefs in International Relations

SpringerBriefs present concise summaries of cutting-edge research and practical applications across a wide spectrum of fields. Featuring compact volumes of 50 to 125 pages, the series covers a range of content from professional to academic. Typical topics might include:

A timely report of state-of-the art analytical techniques

A bridge between new research results, as published in journal articles, and a contextual literature review

A snapshot of a hot or emerging topic

An in-depth case study or clinical example

A presentation of core concepts that students must understand in order to make independent contributions

SpringerBriefs in International Relations showcase emerging theory, empirical research, and practical application in all areas of international relations from a global author community. Topics include, but are not limited to, IR-theory, international security studies, foreign policy, peace and conflict studies, international organization, global governance, international political economy, the history of international relations and related fields.

SpringerBriefs are characterized by fast, global electronic dissemination, standard publishing contracts, standardized manuscript preparation and formatting guidelines, and expedited production schedules.

Hideaki Shinoda · Pavlo Fedorchenko-Kutuyev
Editors

The Impacts of the Russo-Ukrainian War

Theoretical and Practical Explorations
of Policy Agendas for Peace in Ukraine

Editors
Hideaki Shinoda
Graduate School of Global Studies
Tokyo University of Foreign Studies
Fuchu-shi, Tokyo, Japan

Pavlo Fedorchenko-Kutuyev
Igor Sikorsky Kyiv Polytechnic Institute
Kyiv, Ukraine

ISSN 2731-3352 ISSN 2731-3360 (electronic)
SpringerBriefs in International Relations
ISBN 978-981-96-2294-8 ISBN 978-981-96-2295-5 (eBook)
https://doi.org/10.1007/978-981-96-2295-5

© The Editor(s) (if applicable) and The Author(s), under exclusive license to Springer Nature Singapore Pte Ltd. 2025. This book is an open access publication.

Open Access This book is licensed under the terms of the Creative Commons Attribution-NonCommercial-NoDerivatives 4.0 International License (http://creativecommons.org/licenses/by-nc-nd/4.0/), which permits any noncommercial use, sharing, distribution and reproduction in any medium or format, as long as you give appropriate credit to the original author(s) and the source, provide a link to the Creative Commons license and indicate if you modified the licensed material. You do not have permission under this license to share adapted material derived from this book or parts of it.

The images or other third party material in this book are included in the book's Creative Commons license, unless indicated otherwise in a credit line to the material. If material is not included in the book's Creative Commons license and your intended use is not permitted by statutory regulation or exceeds the permitted use, you will need to obtain permission directly from the copyright holder.

This work is subject to copyright. All commercial rights are reserved by the author(s), whether the whole or part of the material is concerned, specifically the rights of translation, reprinting, reuse of illustrations, recitation, broadcasting, reproduction on microfilms or in any other physical way, and transmission or information storage and retrieval, electronic adaptation, computer software, or by similar or dissimilar methodology now known or hereafter developed. Regarding these commercial rights a non-exclusive license has been granted to the publisher.

The use of general descriptive names, registered names, trademarks, service marks, etc. in this publication does not imply, even in the absence of a specific statement, that such names are exempt from the relevant protective laws and regulations and therefore free for general use.

The publisher, the authors and the editors are safe to assume that the advice and information in this book are believed to be true and accurate at the date of publication. Neither the publisher nor the authors or the editors give a warranty, expressed or implied, with respect to the material contained herein or for any errors or omissions that may have been made. The publisher remains neutral with regard to jurisdictional claims in published maps and institutional affiliations.

This Springer imprint is published by the registered company Springer Nature Singapore Pte Ltd.
The registered company address is: 152 Beach Road, #21-01/04 Gateway East, Singapore 189721, Singapore

If disposing of this product, please recycle the paper.

Introduction

This volume is a unique collection of articles authored by Ukrainian and Japanese scholars, focusing on the impacts of the Russo-Ukrainian War. Researchers from both Ukraine and Japan have collaborated for over a year through the "Theory and Practice of Conflict Resolution" (TPCR) study group, organized under the Research Center for Advanced Science and Technology Open Laboratory for Emergence Strategies (ROLES) at the University of Tokyo, Japan. We have regularly conducted research meetings, some held in Kyiv and Tokyo, while others took place online. This volume represents the outcomes of those discussions.[1]

While we share a common academic goal of analyzing the impacts of the Russo-Ukrainian War, we do not necessarily subscribe to a unified ideological stance or advocate any specific policy orientation. Given that the chapters were almost finished before the U.S. presidential election in November 2024, we do not intend to speculate the immediate outcome of the War. Although we are deeply concerned about the situation in Ukraine, especially after the war's outbreak, we recognize the existence of diverse perspectives on how to evaluate its effects. We do not claim that this volume provides a comprehensive examination of all possible approaches. However, by addressing several key points, we aim to offer our insights on the war's impacts to readers who share our concerns.

At the core of our inquiry is the fundamental question: What are the impacts of the Russo-Ukrainian War? This question encompasses both the immediate difficulties Ukraine faces and the challenges of building peace in the post-war period. Rather than focusing on the constantly shifting battlefield maps or making predictions about the war's conclusion—an endeavor too uncertain at present—we aim to offer fundamental perspectives on the war's impacts by identifying key structural and conceptual issues. The agendas range from topics such as the naming of the war, the transformation of the conflict from an internal to an international one, and shifts in both domestic and international perceptions, to regional security mechanisms and the application of theoretical perspectives on conflict resolution, such as concepts of ripeness, balance, and legitimacy.

---

[1] For the activities of our study group, please consult its website. (ROLES TPCR, 2024).

Since Russia's full-scale invasion of Ukraine in February 2022, Japan has emerged as one of Ukraine's most steadfast supporters. Although Japan has refrained from providing lethal weapons—unlike many European and North American allies—it has made substantial contributions in humanitarian and development aid. By June 2024, the Japanese government had provided a total of USD 12 billion in aid, making it the fifth-largest donor to Ukraine, following the USA, UK, Germany, and France. This substantial contribution, notable for an Asian country, reflects Japan's typical levels of Overseas Development Assistance (ODA). Public attention in Japan toward the Russo-Ukrainian War has also been relatively high, particularly when compared to other global armed conflicts.[2] Shortly after Russia's full-scale invasion, Japan decided to significantly increase its defense budget from 1% to 2% of its GDP. In response to the public's shock over the invasion, Japan is re-evaluating its defense policies.

This heightened attention underscores the importance of research into the war's impacts. Unfortunately, opportunities for collaboration between Japanese and Ukrainian scholars, particularly since the full-scale invasion, have been limited. This volume represents a rare attempt at such collaboration, bringing together Japanese and Ukrainian researchers to explore these critical issues.

For the Ukrainian contributors, this collaboration provides a rare opportunity to work with foreign researchers during an ongoing war, which imposes severe travel restrictions. This initiative with Japanese colleagues has enabled regular discussions with foreign researchers, helping Ukrainian academics apply their expertise in response to the crisis. Their dedication is reflected in this volume.

The book is divided into two parts. Part I, *Agendas of the Impacts of the Russo-Ukrainian War*, focuses on key issues that warrant close attention. Defining the current conflict between Russia and Ukraine poses conceptual challenges, prompting broader questions about the nature of modern armed conflicts, which often encompass both international and internal dimensions. We also analyze Ukraine's external environment, including the policies of regional organizations in Europe and the significant transformations within Ukrainian society. Part II, *Agendas for Durable Peace in Ukraine*, takes a broader view, examining theoretical frameworks from sociology, conflict resolution, and international relations, and how these fields apply to the war's impacts.

In Chap. 1, "Problematic Nature of Conceptualizing the Russo-Ukrainian War", the editors outline the foundational perspective on understanding the war. They discuss the problematic nature of terms like "the Ukraine War", which may foster misconceptions about the war's nature. They also explore the political and technical complexities involved in naming any conflict. Chapter 2, "How Do We Approach the Russo-Ukrainian War as an "International Intra-State Armed Conflict"?", examines the question about "international intra-state conflicts" concerning theories of

---

[2] Japan has been providing assistances to Ukraine in the forms of humanitarian and development aid including capacity development through agencies like Japan International Cooperation Agency (JICA) and international organizations, direct financial support, debt suspensions and sanctions of financial measures and visa restrictions (MOFA Japan, 2024).

Conflict Resolution and International Relations. Raising a fundamental question about the distinction between internal and international wars is relevant to the Russo-Ukrainian War. Many contemporary conflicts do not neatly fit into either category, and the Russo-Ukrainian War is one such example. Recognizing this complexity is a starting point for conceptual and theoretical discussions about the war.

Chapter 3, "The International Implications of the Russo-Ukrainian War", investigates the political impacts of the conflict across various regions, detailing how each region has absorbed the war's significant impacts. Chapter 4, "The Impact of the Russo-Ukrainian War on NATO: Implications for the Strategic Concept of the Alliance", highlights the profound effects of the war on NATO (North Atlantic Treaty Organization), particularly with about Ukraine's potential future accession and suggests the need for a restructured concept of alliance within NATO. Chapter 5, "Shifting Trust: Ukrainian Sentiments Towards Social Institutions Before and During War", illustrates how Ukrainians' trust in social institutions has evolved in response to their experiences of war, providing critical data analyses based on social surveys conducted in Ukraine during the conflict.

Chapter 6, "The Scope of the Ripeness Theory in the Russo-Ukrainian War", explores I. William Zartman's "ripeness" theory, a concept in conflict resolution that considers the timing of war termination and mediation efforts, and applies it to Ukraine's history of armed conflict. Chapter 7, "Security Guarantees as Balancing Ukraine with Russia: Reflections on Geopolitical Theories", examines geopolitical and international relations theories from figures like Halford Mackinder, Karl Haushofer, John Mearsheimer, and Henry Kissinger, particularly the ideas of legitimacy and balance. In response to ongoing policy debates on "security guarantees" for Ukraine, this chapter argues that a balanced approach in Ukraine's regional dynamics is central to developing effective security guarantees. Chapter 8, "Community Resilience in Conflict Zones: Identifying Key Factors for Conflict Resolution and Recovery Potential", discusses how Ukrainian communities have built resilience amid the conflict. The chapter shares important findings on how these communities have withstood challenging environments during the war.

In discussing these various topics, the authors do not necessarily seek to provide a coherent set of policy recommendations for the future. Instead, the aim of this book is to contribute academically by offering critical insights into the key issues facing Ukraine and its international partners. We hope that our efforts will stimulate further discussions on the critical impacts of this tragic war.

Hideaki Shinoda
hshinoda@tufs.ac.jp

Pavlo Fedorchenko-Kutuyev

References

TPCR ROLES (2024). Theory and Practice of Conflict Resolution (TPCR) Study Group, organized under the Research Center for Advanced Science and Technology Open Laboratory for Emergence Strategies (ROLES) at the University of Tokyo, Japan. https://roles.rcast.u-tokyo.ac.jp/en/working_group/181, accessed 15 October 2024.

MOFA Japan (2024). Ministry of Foreign Affairs of Japan, Response to the Situation in Ukraine https://www.mofa.go.jp/erp/c_see/ua/page3e_001171.html, accessed 15 October 2024.

Contents

Part I Agendas of the Impacts of the Russo-Ukrainian War

1. **Problematic Nature of Conceptualizing the Russo-Ukrainian War** 3
   Pavlo Fedorchenko-Kutuyev and Hideaki Shinoda

2. **How Do We Approach the Russo-Ukrainian War as an "International Intra-State Armed Conflict"?** 13
   Hideaki Shinoda

3. **The International Implications of the Russo-Ukrainian War** 27
   Iurii Perga

4. **The Impact of the Russo-Ukrainian War on NATO: Implications for the Strategic Concept of the Alliance** 43
   Tomonori Yoshizaki and Hideaki Shinoda

5. **Shifting Trust: Ukrainian Sentiments Towards Social Institutions Before and During War** 59
   Olena Akimova and Anna Ishchenko

Part II Agendas for Durable Peace in Ukraine

6. **The Scope of the Ripeness Theory in the Russo-Ukrainian War** 71
   Hinako Yasui and Hideaki Shinoda

7. **Security Guarantees as Balancing Ukraine with Russia: Reflections on Geopolitical Theories** 81
   Hideaki Shinoda

8 **Community Resilience in Conflict Zones: Identifying Key Factors for Conflict Resolution and Recovery Potential** 101
Olena Akimova, Anna Ishchenko, and Iurii Perga

Conclusion: The Russo–Ukrainian War and Global Order Melting into the Air? 119

Editors and Contributors

About the Editors

Hideaki Shinoda is Professor at Institute of Global Studies, Tokyo University of Foreign Studies (TUFS) and Visiting Senior Research Fellow, ROLES University of Tokyo. He obtained a Ph.D. in International Relations at the London School of Economics and Political Science (LSE). After working as a part-time teacher at LSE and Keele University, he took a research fellow position at the Institute for Peace Science of Hiroshima University, where he became Associate Professor. Then, he took the current position at the Tokyo University of Foreign Studies in 2013. He has been a visiting scholar at the Lauterpacht Research Centre for International Law, Cambridge University (2000) and at the Center for the Study of Human Rights, Columbia University (2002). He was Visiting Professional at the International Criminal Court (2017). He is the author of many books and articles including *Partnership Peace Operations: UN and Regional Organizations in Multiple Layers of International Security* (Routledge, 2024). He has received academic awards including Osaragi Jiro Rondan Award (2003), Suntory Academic Award (2012), Yomiuri Yoshino Sakuzo Award (2017).

Pavlo Fedorchenko-Kutuyev is Professor of Sociology and Sociology Department Chair at Igor Sikorsky Kyiv Polytechnic Institute (KPI). His career highlights include Professor of Sociology and Sociology Department Chair, Igor Sikorsky Kyiv Polytechnic Institute (2013–Present), Visiting Scholar at prestigious institutions such as Stanford University (USA), University of Tokyo (Japan), St. John's College (Oxford University, UK), and others. Deputy Editor-in-Chief of KPI Journal of Sociology, Political Science, and Law (2013–Present), Executive Director of the Center for Comparative Politics, a Ukrainian non-governmental think tank (1993–1999). His areas of specialties are History of Sociology, Historical Sociology, Contemporary sociological theory, Sociology of development and modernization, Political Sociology, Conflict Resolution. He also has published some teaching manuals and 75 textbooks and articles.

Contributors

Anna Ishchenko is Senior Lecturer and Deputy Dean of FSP for international activities, Igor Sikorsky Kyiv Polytechnic Institute (KPI). She has had an internship at Masaryk University Training Week (MUST Week) under the Erasmus+ program, Scientific and Practical Seminar: "Qualitative Methods in Sociological Research" (Higher School of Sociology at the Institute of Sociology of the National Academy of Sciences of Ukraine) and currently the Director of the Scientific Research Center of Applied Sociology "Sotsioplus". Field of Scientific Interests are Applied Sociology, Factors of Formation and Development of Human Capital, Philosophy of Education and Expert Research Methods

Olena Akimova is Docent and Acting Dean of the Faculty of Sociology and Law, Igor Sikorsky Kyiv Polytechnic Institute (KPI). She has teaching experience at the "Igor Sikorsky Kyiv Polytechnic Institute" from 2016 to present at the Department of Management Theory and Practice, Department of Philosophy and Department of Sociology and Law, KPI. Her areas of interests are Higher Education like Policy Analysis, Public governance, Sustainability and Information Society. Some of her publications include Improvement of Ways of Human Capital Development as a Factor of Increase Mobilization Potential of Ukraine: Monograph, Management in the sphere of education and science to ensure the sustainable development of the state and regions. She has over 50 scientific publications and co-authors, 11 collective publications and 14 articles.

Iurii Perga is Associate Professor and Vice-Dean for Research and Innovation, Igor Sikorsky Kyiv Polytechnic Institute [KPI]. He obtained Master's degree at Taras Shevchenko National University of Kyiv and Ph.D. at National Technical University of Ukraine "Kyiv Polytechnic Institute" Wroclaw University Candidate of Historical Sciences. He has had internship with the University of Warsaw, Bergen-Belsen Memorial, and Vytautas Magnus University. His interests are Ukrainian-Polish relations in the first half of the twentieth century and history of ICT development in the EU. He also published 20+ scientific publications.

Hinako Yasui is a graduate student at Graduate School of Public Policy (GraSPP), the University of Tokyo. She specializes in conflict resolution, especially Ripeness Theory. In her undergraduate era, she belonged to research group of Peacebuilding.

Tomonori Yoshizaki is Professor at Institute of Global Studies, Tokyo University for Foreign Studies (TUFS). He was Vice President for Academic Affairs of Japan MoD's National Institute for Defense Studies (NIDS). At NIDS, He was Director of Policy Simulation (2015–22), and Director of Security Studies Department (2011–2015) at NIDS. He has been regularly attending NATO Defense College Conference of Commandants (COC), and ASEAN Regional Forum (ARF) Meeting of Head of National Defense Universities/Colleges/Institutions. He is currently a visiting professor/lecture at Self-Defense Forces Staff Colleges, Tokyo University for Foreign Studies, and National Graduate Institute for Policy Studies (GRIPS).

Previously, he was an assistant director of Office of Strategic Studies of MoD, a visiting scholar at Kings College London, and Hudson Institute; His areas of expertise include alliance management, European security and NATO, Japan's security policy and peace operations.

Part I
Agendas of the Impacts of the Russo-Ukrainian War

Chapter 1
Problematic Nature of Conceptualizing the Russo-Ukrainian War

Pavlo Fedorchenko-Kutuyev and Hideaki Shinoda

Contents

1.1	The Problem of the Phrase "Ukraine War"	3
1.2	Reflections on the Use of the Phrase "Ukraine War"	8
References		10

Abstract The widely circulated phrases like "Ukraine War" or "Ukrainian War" are politically problematic and conceptually misleading. The Russo-Ukrainian War involves Russia as a major conflict party, which should be addressed correctly. Political propaganda could manipulate misleading names. There are three major patterns of naming wars; highlighting conflict parties, particular characteristics, and geographical locations. Some of the recent wars were indeed named after geographical locations, as in the case of the "Iraq War". But they are also problematic in their nature of hiding major conflict parties, even starters of their wars.

Keywords Russo-Ukrainian war · Russia's invasion of Ukraine · Ukraine war · Naming wars · Propaganda · Iraq war · Global war on terror (GWOT)

1.1 The Problem of the Phrase "Ukraine War"

War is the continuation of politics by other means, a famous saying goes. In the second section of this piece, we examined the complexities surrounding the term "Ukraine War" from both international law and international relations perspectives. If we look at Russian aggression against Ukraine through the lens of *realpolitik*, addressing the issue of public opinion becomes essential. Winning on the battlefield is essential for Ukraine's survival, both politically and physically, given the genocidal

---

P. Fedorchenko-Kutuyev
Igor Sikorsky Kyiv Polytechnic Institute, Kyiv, Ukraine

H. Shinoda (✉)
Tokyo University of Foreign Studies, Tokyo, Japan
e-mail: hshinoda@tufs.ac.jp

© The Author(s) 2025
H. Shinoda and P. Ferdorchenko-Kutuyev (eds.),
The Impacts of the Russo-Ukrainian War, SpringerBriefs in International Relations,
https://doi.org/10.1007/978-981-96-2295-5_1

nature of Russian aggression. However, the war is a multifaceted undertaking, and it is taking place within political context. Consequently, it is critical for Ukraine's defense strategy to secure political victories, which necessitates garnering support in the court of public opinion. Mass media plays an important role in informing the public and public opinion in both senses of the word "inform"—providing information (facts, data, etc.) and influencing/shaping the public's views and opinions.

Thus, the choice of words/terms to describe Russia's invasion of Ukraine is extremely significant and consequential. Although reputable media outlets use precise terms like "Russia-Ukraine War," they also deem it acceptable to use the shorthand "Ukraine War" in their titles. This is a major problem, as the latter expression obscures the nature of Russia's aggression against Ukraine. The situation is worsened by Russia's aggressive, adept, and lavishly funded global propaganda machine which disseminates false narratives about Ukraine. Key messages from this propaganda include claims questioning the illegitimacy of the Ukrainian government after the Maidan revolution that ousted Russian puppet Victor Yanukovch, assertions about the artificial nature of the Ukrainian nation, and allegations of a Nazi presence in Ukrainian politics. Russian propaganda adeptly engages with the paranoid rhetoric of populist demagogues in liberal democracies—such as the Trumpist movement—in an attempt to legitimize and sanitize its war against Ukraine. It is worth noting that the Russian state also actively leverages the Orthodox Church to advance its agenda on a global scale. Given the sheer scale of atrocities committed by Russians against Ukrainians during this phase of war against Ukraine, it is imperative for Ukraine to disseminate accurate information about the Russo-Ukrainian war. The key element of this strategy is calling a spade a spade. The Russian war on Ukraine should be accurately portrayed and understood for what it is—an unprovoked and unlawful act of aggression. Ukrainian academics and diplomatic missions should take a central role in spreading accurate information about this war, in order to win public opinion and secure support from as many national governments as possible, with the aim of ending the war on terms favorable to Ukraine.

According to Charles Tilly's famous dictum to wage wars states require two strong arms—the tax authority to raise money to finance the war on the one hand and the ministry of war on the other. Contemporary states alongside the military hardware, economic resources and administrative capacity employ soft power. (Nye, 2004) Eminent British historian of global conflicts remarked in his seminal study of rise and fall of great powers that although a nation's GDP matters, wars aren't won by economic indicators alone. (Kennedy, 1987, pp. xxv, 677) In the same vein wars require more than just military hardware and a vast amount of soldiers. The importance of soft power—the ability of the state to project its attractive image regionally and globally and in such a way advance its (material) national interests and international political goals—should never be underestimated. Soft power and hard power are tensely intertwined and are mutually reinforcing. Abundant economy helps finance the culture and its global promotion. The culture in turn improves the image of the state to the point of whitewashing it from aggressive actions and even crimes. This is exactly what Russia has been doing in the context of the Russo-Ukrainian war. It has been weaponizing its cultural heritage, the language and cultural influence as well as potent tools of propaganda, which in turn aims—sometimes successfully—at shaping public opinion. After all, culture is about defining and naming reality. A recent presentation by Liubov Tsybulska—an expert from The Ukrainian Institute—poignantly titled "Shorts of Love" reveals how the Russian culture war machine works.[1] It's also worth noting that it is hard for a nation fighting for its very existence to spend enough resources on disseminating the facts about atrocities it suffers as a result of aggression.

War as an armed conflict between states has always included not just clash of armies, navies and air forces but the war of words—also known as information/propaganda warfare—as well. And these efforts on the Russia side have been paying off. The study of the Russian propaganda influence on Americans has revealed that it does have an effect on its recipients in the area which matters the most for Ukraine, that of the US foreign policy. After an exposure to Russian government state propaganda outlet RT respondents approval of the US foreign policy stoked by 10%; republicans turned out to be even more susceptible to the sway of Russian narratives (Carter and Carter 2021, pp. 49–78).

If we look at the facts, the aggressive and atrocious nature of the Russian war on Ukraine is self-evident. Having been laying ground for attack against Ukraine for decades, Russia employed its armed forces in 2014 to occupy Ukrainian territories—Crimea and parts of Donetsk and Luhansk regions. After decades of neglect Ukrainian armed and security forces were in disarray (Stanislav, 2024) and allowed generally bloodless seizure of Crimea by Russian forces, yet put up a stiff fight in Eastern Ukraine. Then 8 years of protracted localized violence took place between two belligerents—Ukrainian armed forces on the one hand and Russia organized, backed and armed eastern Ukrainian paramilitaries with frequent involvement of Russian regular troops on the other. That situation fits into Hobbes' understanding of war: "War consisteth not in battle only, or the act of fighting; but in a tract of time, wherein the will to contend by battle is as sufficiently known" (Hobbes, 1914, p. 64).

On February 24, 2022 Russia launched a totally unprovoked invasion of the Ukrainian proper. Yet, both before and during this Russian aggressive war against Ukraine, the military attacks have been accompanied by a massive war of words—extremely well-funded by the Russian state propaganda warfare against Ukraine. This fake news onslaught is aimed at the Russian populace, Ukrainians and global audiences. Russia is massively investing into propaganda/disinformation/fake news. The Russian government infamous international media outlet "Russia Today" is projected to receive around USD 300 million in state funding, while weekly governmental expenditures on propaganda will amount to USD 27 million, amounting to USD 1.42 billion for the year 2025. (Artemchuk, 2024) Apart from media outlets Russia maintains a vast network of diplomatic missions worldwide making it number 6 with 230 posts in 230 cities in Global diplomacy index country ranking.[2]

Although information warfare/propaganda are usually viewed as essential to hybrid warfare, they have been an indispensable part of "conventional" wars and

---

[1] https://www.instagram.com/p/DBMKzrWN2rZ/?igsh=ZGttYzc3NWUxZndr.

[2] https://globaldiplomacyindex.lowyinstitute.org/.

geopolitical conflicts/rivalry. Let's look at Sino-American relations. They are a case in point as far as the influence of information hostilities on the dynamics of public opinion is concerned.

It is worth noting that theory and politics of modernization in post-World War II America was focusing on two mutually reinforcing processes—promoting developmental addenda and winning hearts and minds of the Third World nations, thus ensuring their gravitation towards the US-led order instead of being seduced by the Soviet Leninist regime promise of radiant future.

As we have mentioned above, quite a few nations on the Global South are preoccupied with their own challenges and priorities which mainly revolve around the economic and national security of these states. Thus, quite a few nations are helping Russia circumvent the sanctions by supplying it with dual use technologies and thus fueling the Russian war machine.

Russian aggression is the war of survival for Ukraine as a country and Ukrainians as a nation. Many other nations, especially those belonging to a so-called Global South, view Russo-Ukrainian war as just one of the numerous armed conflicts and disasters ravaging around the world and disproportionately affecting poor heavily indebted nations.

Influential Indian foreign policy official and scholar Sivshankar Menon has worded the issue succinctly in his piece in Foreign Affairs: "The multisided competition and great-power rivalry have led many countries in the global South to be unaligned rather than nonaligned, dissociated from the present order and seeking their own independent solutions rather than an alternative set of widely held approaches to global issues. Disillusioned by great-power rivalry, many countries are seeking their own solutions. Alienated and resentful, many developing countries see the war in Ukraine and the West's rivalry with China as distracting from urgent issues such as debt, climate change, and the effects of the pandemic. Take South Asia. Three countries in the region—Bangladesh, Pakistan, and Sri Lanka—have been in talks with the IMF for more than a year about adjustment packages to deal with their debt. And over the last 18 months, five countries in the region—Afghanistan, Myanmar, Nepal, Pakistan, and Sri Lanka—have also changed governments, and not always smoothly or constitutionally. Sri Lanka defaulted on its international debts in April 2022. During the summer, one-fifth of Pakistan's population was rendered homeless by floods inundating one-third of the country—a devastating consequence of climate change. Neither international institutions, nor the West, nor its Chinese and Russian rivals, have found or offered meaningful solutions to these problems" (Menon, 2023).

Russian propaganda is good at red herring tactics diverting attention to insignificant and/or irrelevant issues, while concealing the genocidal and criminal nature of the Russian war against Ukrainians.

The fall of communist regimes—the "Leninist extinction" as US Berkeley political scientist Ken Jowitt vividly put it (Ken, 1993)—heralded the transition from the Cold War global order to something new. Crudely put, two conflicting schools of thought emerged to tackle the new reality—end of history thesis vs. clash civilizations. As world affairs unfolded it appeared that the grim interpretation of state of the world has more merit than an optimistic one. The recent decade has been a witness to a brazen challenge to imperfect yet habitual rules of the global engagements. In 2014 Russia invaded Ukraine having occupied Crimea and parts of eastern Ukraine. That was a focal point that might be a defining moment of the twenty-first century. In February 2022 Russia launched a full-scale invasion of Ukraine. Russia is one of the biggest nuclear powers, it enjoys the permanent membership in the UN Security Council and its leader has officially branded the demise of the Soviet Union as the biggest geopolitical catastrophe of the twentieth century. Therefore, Russia's war against Ukraine goes beyond the framework of the regional conflict and poses a global threat. Prior to the full-scale invasion of Ukraine, Russia presented its list of demands to NATO, demanding that NATO roll back its pre-1997 boundaries (that would exclude/strip off the membership of countries like East and Central European Nations.

Clear definitions are critical elements of the research. Definitions also indispensable for policy making as a tool helping navigate through tumultuous waters of the world (dis)order. Thus names/definitions matter. They also matter in the global court of global opinion. Who's the aggressor and who's the victim of aggression? Who rightfully defends one's sovereignty and exercises the sovereign nation's right to join European and Euro-Atlantic institutions who's hell bent on derailing these efforts even at the cost of genocidely obliterating its neighbor? These are not just rhetorical questions. At the time of the war—and Russia's full scale aggression against Ukraine is the biggest war in Europe since World War II—these are issues of life and death for hundreds of thousands of Ukrainians.

Precise definitions and distinctions in Pierre Bourdieu's fashion (see his seminal Distinctions) between villains and forces of good help dismantle webs of lies promoted by the Russian state and its agents/proxies worldwide and thus mobilize global support for the cause of Ukrainian sovereign and democratic development. The testimony to the power of words is the story of the renewal of the US military aid to Ukraine.

Lifeline from the US to Ukrainian military was renewed from having been buried in the gridlock in the US House of Representatives after the personal meeting of the speaker of the House with a fellow baptist church goer from Ukraine who shared his personal story of losing his wife and son to a Russian drone attack on civilian quitters of city of Odessa (Vorozhko, 2024).

Having outlined the critical importance of calling a spade a spade, in other words calling a Russian aggression against Ukraine a Russian war on Ukraine we will proceed with more empirically oriented discussion of the word usage in describing/defining armed conflicts/wars. War is the continuation of politics by other means, a famous saying goes. In the second section of this piece, we examine the complexities surrounding the term "Ukraine War" from both international law and international relations perspectives.

1.2 Reflections on the Use of the Phrase "Ukraine War"

Governments throughout the world officially do not use the phrases "Ukrainian War" or "Ukraine War".[3] As a result, international organizations like the UN likewise do not use such naming conventions for the conflict. Many states and international organizations are more precise in their references to the war, describing it as a "Russia's full-scale invasion of Ukraine" or "Russian aggression" to accurately convey the legal context of the situation. These entities are also apparently aware of the problematic nature of the phrase, "Ukrainian War". In order to avoid the political connotations, governments and international organizations simply avoid using the phrase. Despite the political sensitivity, however, journalists and even scholars so often carelessly use the phrase; the reason being that it is simple and an editor can reduce the number of words in titles. However, the choice of phrasing may inadvertently reflect a political stance, which those using the phrase may or may not intend. The phrase, "Ukrainian War", may be chosen for its journalistic impact to quickly catch the reader's attention. Beyond this commercial rationale, there also seem to be some conventional reasons behind the scenes, which carry sensitive political implications. In order to identify the problematic nature of the expression, let us explore three major patterns of the way we name wars.

First, the traditional manner of naming a war is to use the names of the two warring states. This custom became prevalent around the nineteenth century during the times of great power politics and after the establishment of international law based upon the concept of state sovereignty. For instance, when Japan waged war against Russia in 1904, the war was called "Russo-Japanese War". In this way, many scholars are now using the expression "Russo-Ukrainian War" to describe the ongoing war between Russia and Ukraine as objectively as possible.

Second, when the number of warring parties are so numerous that mentioning only a few would be misleading, the task of naming the war becomes problematic. Typical examples are the "First World War" or the "Thirty Years War", etc. Similarly, a series of wars may be described using various terms, such as the war known in Israel as the "Yom Kippur War, which is referred to in the Arab World as the "October War". This approach to naming has not been applied to the ongoing war between Russia and Ukraine. Although NATO member states are currently offering strong support to Ukraine, they are not actually parties to the conflict. In addition, there is no clear consensus on any culturally symbolic or period-descriptive characteristics of the war that inform how it is so referred.

Third, a war sometimes carries the name of a particular geographical area especially when the geographical location is related to the vital war agenda. Classic examples would include the "Crimean War" or "Falkland Islands War (Conflict)". Since the end of WWII in 1945, the majority of armed conflicts have been intra-state wars. As a result, it has become increasingly common to name wars after the specific

---

[3] The government of Russia uses the phrase "Special Military Operation". It is supposed be because of concerns about domestic legal settings as well as domestic public opinion, which does not necessarily reflect the nature of the war. So this chapter does not examine the phrase.

geographical regions where the armed conflicts take place, such as the "Biafran War" or the "Tigray Conflict". This naming convention is also seen in inter-state wars, particularly when the conflict arises from a territorial dispute, as in the cases of the "Kashmir Conflict" or the "Cyprus Conflict". When a civil war encompasses nearly the entire geographical territory of a sovereign state, the conflict is often named after the state itself, as in examples like the "Sierra Leone Civil War" or the "Liberian Civil War".

When the United States labeled its 2001 military campaign against the Taliban in Afghanistan the "Afghanistan War", and its 2003 invasion of Iraq as the "Iraq War", it was employing the third pattern of war naming. They named the war after the name of the state where the war took place geographically. After 1945, the United States has consistently used this geographical naming pattern in its 20th-century military engagements, as seen in conflicts like the "Korean War" and the "Vietnam War". Yet, these wars had the structure of the confrontation between the same national groups before active U.S. involvement. It can be said that the U.S. only intervened in wars between the same national groups, even if its intervention may have intensified the wars significantly. The "Bosnian Conflict" and the "Kosovo Conflict" involved U.S. intervention in civil wars via NATO, either with the backing or under scrutiny of the UN Security Council. In the case of the 2001 Afghanistan War, it is important to note that a civil war had already been ongoing in Afghanistan prior to the U.S. invasion. However, we typically make a distinction between the civil war in Afghanistan before 2001 and the conflict initiated by the U.S. in 2001. In the case of the "Iraq War" of 2003, it was more clearly the case that the U.S. started the war by invading Iraq. There had been no substantively continuous civil war in Iraq before the US invasion.[4]

The George W. Bush administration liked to use the phrase, the "Global War on Terror (GWOT)", which served as a sweeping, rhetorical characterization of global conflict under the Bush Doctrine's "you're either with us or without us" stance. Yet if the two wars in Afghanistan and Iraq were geographically confined wars in the larger GWOT, it could have been possible that the two wars were treated as territorial wars of a larger war, rather than just wars between sovereign states. Nevertheless, the GWOT was in the end such an abstract war that the argument would not sound sufficiently plausible. In fact, most international lawyers today consider the "Iraq War" or the "US invasion of Iraq" as an unlawful act of aggression. The choice between the two possible names for the same event is inherently tied to our assessment of the legality of the U.S. action in 2003.

It is here that the very problematic nature of the phrasing of the "Ukraine War" appears. If we refer to the U.S. action in 2003 the "Iraq War", rather than the "U.S. aggression in Iraq" or even the "U.S.-Iraq War", it opens the door for accepting Russia's argument that their "special military operation" is a fight against "oppression by the Neo-Nazi regime in Kyiv" and the "imperial expansion of NATO." This

---

[4] Hideaki Shinoda argued in 2003 that the only possibility of justification of the US invasion in Iraq is humanitarian intervention. If we took human rights abuse by the regime of Saddam Hussein seriously, we could identify the elements of the confrontation between the regime and the Iraqi people and argue that the US only intervened in the conflict. But this is a weak argument that cannot be easily justified in contemporary international law (Shinoda, 2003; Shinoda, 2023).

argument is used to justify protecting the Russian speaking population's "war of independence" in parts of Ukraine (originally limited to Donetsk, Luhansk, and Crimea, but now also including Zaporizhzhia and Kherson, which Russia eventually aims to annex). The vast majority of countries globally avoid using the term "Ukraine War", at least officially. This is because approximately three-quarters of UN General Assembly members voted in favor of a resolution recognizing Russia's actions as "aggression", which is inherently illegal under international law and violates the UN Charter. Notably, those who use the phrase, the "Ukrainian War" or "Ukraine War", are challenging this subtle yet significant standpoint in favor of Russia to the detriment of Ukraine.

The phrase, "Ukraine War", is truly problematic legally and politically. The U.S., which is responsible for the invasion in Iraq in 2003, is now a major supporter of Ukraine. The U.S. government, however, is cautious in its terminology, deliberately avoiding the use of the phrases "Ukraine War" or "Ukrainian War", to highlight the illegality of Russia's actions in Ukraine. Nonetheless, many Americans, including journalists and scholars, freely use the terms "Ukraine War" or "Ukrainian War", seemingly without questioning the implications of such naming, as they did with the "Iraq War". Those hesitant to challenge popular American sentiment may avoid questioning the problematic nature of the phrases, the "Ukraine War" as well as the "Iraq War". In doing so, they inadvertently align with President Vladimir Putin's narrative, which frames Russia's actions as a "special military operation" in Ukraine's so-called war of independence.

Should proponents of the "Global South" against the "Global North" or those with anti-US or anti-Western ideologies begin to argue for replacing the term "Iraq War" with something equivalent to the "U.S. full-scale invasion of Iraq", many Americans may find themselves perplexed. The problematic nature of the phrase "Ukraine War", which is not something more equivalent to "Russia's full-scale invasion of Ukraine", really entails highly controversial and deeply political issues. One may find it intimidating to discuss the issue. Nevertheless, a heightened academic awareness is essential for a more nuanced analysis of the nature of the ongoing war and its broader context.

References

Artemchuk, O. (2024, October 7). *Russia to increase propaganda spending to historic high of $27 million per week.* (https://www.pravda.com.ua/eng/news/2024/10/7/7478539/)
Carter, E. B., & Carter, B. L. (2021). Questioning more: RT, outward-facing propaganda, and the post-west world order. *Security Studies, 30*(1), 49–78.
Hobbes, T. (1914). *The Leviathan.* The Aldme Press.
Ken, J. (1993). *New world disorder: The Leninist extinction.* UC Press.
Kennedy, P. (1987). *The rise and fall of the great powers: Economic change and military conflict from 1500 to 2000.* Random House.

Menon, S. (2023). *Out of alignment what the war in Ukraine has revealed about non-western powers*. Foreign Affairs. (https://www.foreignaffairs.com/world/out-alignment-war-in-ukraine-non-western-powers-shivshankar-menon)

Nye, J. S. (2004). *Soft power: The means to success in world politics*. Public Affairs.

Shinoda, H. (2003). *Peacebuilding and the rule of law (Heiwakochiku to Honoshihai)*. Tokyo: Sobunsha (Japanese).

Shinoda, H. (2023). The impact of the global war on terrorism upon international peace operations. *Kosaikankeironso, 12*(1), 19–34.

Stanislav, A. (2024). *Building state capacity: The impact of armed conflict and external threats on social and political transformations in Ukraine (in Ukrainian)*. MA dissertation in sociology. KPI. https://ela.kpi.ua/items/6fa59299-55c6-4db5-baad-161dce9e89e6

Vorozhko, T. (2024). *Statistics, prayer, personal stories: How protestants helped bring Ukraine aid to US house floor*. https://www.holosameryky.com/a/statistics-prayer-personal-stories-how-protestants-helped-bring-ukraine-aid-to-us-house-floor-/7601300.html

Open Access This chapter is licensed under the terms of the Creative Commons Attribution-NonCommercial-NoDerivatives 4.0 International License (http://creativecommons.org/licenses/by-nc-nd/4.0/), which permits any noncommercial use, sharing, distribution and reproduction in any medium or format, as long as you give appropriate credit to the original author(s) and the source, provide a link to the Creative Commons license and indicate if you modified the licensed material. You do not have permission under this license to share adapted material derived from this chapter or parts of it.

The images or other third party material in this chapter are included in the chapter's Creative Commons license, unless indicated otherwise in a credit line to the material. If material is not included in the chapter's Creative Commons license and your intended use is not permitted by statutory regulation or exceeds the permitted use, you will need to obtain permission directly from the copyright holder.

Chapter 2
How Do We Approach the Russo-Ukrainian War as an "International Intra-State Armed Conflict"?

Hideaki Shinoda

Contents

2.1	Introductory Question	14
2.2	The Gap Between Theory of Conflict Resolution and Reality of Armed Conflicts	15
2.3	The Gap Between International Relations and Conflict Resolution	16
2.4	Political Realism and the State-Centric Bias	17
2.5	Theories of Conflict Resolution and the Myth of New Wars	18
2.6	Reflections on the Constraints of Policy Perspectives in Conflict Resolution	21
2.7	Reality of Armed Conflicts in the Contemporary World	22
2.8	Conflict Resolution Policies Need to Be Adjusted	23
2.9	Concluding Remarks	24
References		25

Abstract The phenomenon of "international intra-state armed conflicts" poses serious challenges to the theory and practice of conflict resolution. The distinction between intra-state armed conflicts and international wars has created a strong perception that, while international wars were dominant in the past, most contemporary armed conflicts are intra-state. The disciplinary demarcation between Conflict Resolution and International Relations has resulted in biases that overlook "international intra-state armed conflicts." Given the growing number of such conflicts, the theory and practice of conflict resolution need to transcend the bias stemming from the artificial distinction between international wars and "international intra-state armed conflicts." Integrating deterrence into conflict resolution strategies is essential, as is the combination of international and domestic monitoring mechanisms with the mediation of conflicting parties. Furthermore, peacebuilding assistance should be globally reinforced by incorporating lessons learned from the end of the Cold War and the Global War on Terror. Adopting flexible perspectives, such as those promoted by the Free and Open Indo-Pacific (FOIP) framework, can enhance international partnerships. For instance, Ukraine has the potential to emerge as a maritime

---

H. Shinoda (✉)
Tokyo University of Foreign Studies, Tokyo, Japan
e-mail: hshinoda@tufs.ac.jp

© The Author(s) 2025
H. Shinoda and P. Ferdorchenko-Kutuyev (eds.),
The Impacts of the Russo-Ukrainian War, SpringerBriefs in International Relations,
https://doi.org/10.1007/978-981-96-2295-5_2

power in the Black Sea, connecting the Indo-Pacific region through the Red Sea and the Mediterranean Sea.

Keywords International intra-state conflict · Inter-state conflict · Intra-state conflict · Conflict resolution · International relations · Peacebuilding · Liberal peacebuilding theory · Deterrence · Free and open Indo-Pacific (FOIP)

2.1 Introductory Question

This essay argues that there is a phenomenon of "international intra-state armed conflicts," a concept that may seem complex and contradictory. Conventionally, armed conflicts are categorized as either international or intra-state, not both simultaneously. However, many conflicts exhibit elements of both types. In numerous armed conflicts, multiple domestic actors operate within one sovereign state's territory, often with foreign intervention forces present. The demarcation between internal and international aspects becomes dubious in practice (Davies et al., 2024; UCDP, 2023).

One may say that while an intra-state armed conflict may become internationalized when an external state directly or indirectly gets involved with the conflict, an intra-state conflict remains an intra-state conflict. But it is sometimes the case that an inter-state armed conflict may influence or even create an intra-state conflict. It is often the case that intra-state conflicts and inter-state conflicts are intrinsically interlinked with each other, it is too difficult or artificial to distinguish them clearly. For instance, the wider Gaza crisis involving Israel, Hamas, Hizballah in Lebanon, the Houthi in Yemen, and Iran further illustrates this complexity. The term "international intra-state armed conflicts" is used to convey the multidimensional nature of such conflicts.

This phenomenon poses significant challenges to conflict resolution theory and practice. The conventional distinction between intra-state armed conflicts and international wars is considered convenient but is artificial, leading to a distorted perception of contemporary conflicts. The disciplinary division between Conflict Resolution and International Relations contributes to this bias, as the former focuses on intra-state conflicts and the latter on international conflicts. Given the increasing occurrence of "international intra-state armed conflicts," there is a need to overcome the bias of this artificial distinction.

This chapter casts serious doubt on the simplistic view of the nature of the Russo-Ukrainian War. It is often said that the War is a rare example of inter-state war in the contemporary international community. But the view needs to be contextualized by the observation that the contemporary world is full of "international intra-state armed conflicts". For instance, the Donbas War in eastern Ukraine and Russia's full-scale invasion of the entire country, present theoretical possibilities of demarcation, which eventually proves extremely difficult in practice. One may say that the former started in 2014 and the latter in 2022. But does it mean that the Donbas War disappeared all of sudden as a result of the full-scale invasion? Or the former still now coexists with the latter? Or the former was absorbed into the latter to be one war? These questions deserve serious attention, as they affect the conceptual framework of our understanding of the Russo-Ukrainian War. The battles exist as physical reality. But in the end the perception of armed conflicts is more or less conceptual. From this theoretical or conceptual perspective, this chapter explore the complex nature of the Russo-Ukrainian War.

2.2 The Gap Between Theory of Conflict Resolution and Reality of Armed Conflicts

The theory and practice of conflict resolution developed over the past decades require reexamination in light of numerous armed conflicts with high casualties, many of which are prolonged or reignited. Current approaches have serious shortcomings in analyzing policies designed to alleviate or prevent armed conflicts. Identifying major flaws in the analysis and approaches of conflict resolution is crucial for addressing these challenges.

Behind the challenge there is the challenge of analyzing and addressing "international intra-state armed conflicts". Describing a conflict as both international and intra-state may initially appear contradictory, challenging the traditional distinction between international and intra-state wars. However, the reality is that the contemporary world is rife with armed conflicts exhibiting elements of both types. Many conflicts simultaneously involve international and intra-state dimensions, with the number of such conflicts on the rise.

This phenomenon challenges the simplistic view that conflicts are either international or intra-state. Instead, many contemporary armed conflicts feature both external and domestic actors. The coexistence of international and intra-state elements within the same conflict is becoming increasingly common. In essence, the concept of "international intra-state armed conflicts" is not an exception but a prevalent occurrence in today's armed conflicts. External actors often play a significant role while domestic factions engage in conflict with each other.

There is a myth that recent armed conflicts are mostly intra-state wars, while international armed conflicts were dominant in the past. But the fact is that the number and percentage of intra-state armed conflicts were always high during the Cold War period. After the collapse of the European empires at the end of World War I, followed by the wave of decolonization after World War II, the number of states dramatically increased. The newly independent states born after WWII have continued to provide theatres of armed conflicts, particularly those in which intra-state conflicts occurred. At the same time, these states have shared regional conditions of political, economic, and social fragility with neighboring states, and quite often had international dimensions in conflicts, whether through interventions from or assistance by external actors. Conflicts easily tend to spill over. International intra-state conflicts are not exceptional but normal in our contemporary world.

Despite this reality, theories of conflict resolution have heavily relied on the myth that contemporary armed conflicts are solely intra-state. While focusing on the intra-state nature of contemporary armed conflicts is useful and indispensable, it fails to capture all essential aspects, as many conflicts also possess international dimensions. Given the high number of armed conflicts and the ineffectiveness of international responses, it is necessary to critically reexamine the assumptions underlying conflict resolution theories. This reexamination is crucial to ensure that theoretical insights align with the complex and evolving nature of armed conflicts in the twenty-first century.

2.3 The Gap Between International Relations and Conflict Resolution

Within the field of International Relations, a well-established perspective on the "level of analysis" problem warns against the potential confusion of different analytical layers. This perspective emphasizes the importance of maintaining clear distinctions among the analyses of individuals, the state, and international relations, acknowledging that a single war may have multiple causal dimensions. Despite recognizing the coexistence of intra-state and international elements in armed conflicts, the discipline of International Relations has not consistently applied multidimensional analysis. Instead, the level of analysis problem is often used to justify the exclusivity of the International Relations perspective.

Consequently, a de facto division of labor has emerged. International Relations tends to analyze historical or hypothetical international conflicts, while the field of Conflict Resolution focuses on inter-state conflicts in the contemporary world. The assumption that contemporary armed conflicts are exclusively intra-state has widened the gap between International Relations and Conflict Resolution over the past few decades. Additionally, this division has led to the separation of theorizing international order from analyzing armed conflicts in the contemporary world.

This strict disciplinary division hampers the development of conflict analysis from multiple dimensions. Both International Relations and Conflict Resolution offer unique approaches that could enhance multidimensional conflict analysis. However, the strict disciplinary division prevents the effective integration of these approaches in coherent ways. Studies of international affairs and armed conflicts operate in isolation, often underestimating the impact of changes in international order on armed conflicts and neglecting the influence of intra-state armed conflicts on the course of international order.

The problem of strictly demarcating between international and intra-state armed conflicts results in an inability to recognize the phenomenon of armed conflicts flexibly and realistically. Excluding international elements from intra-state armed conflicts leads to the oversight of their extraterritorial dimensions. The biased assumption that an intra-state conflict is geographically and politically confined within one territorial sovereign state becomes an obstacle in analyzing its complex multidimensional nature.

To overcome this obstacle and the associated perception biases in recognizing armed conflicts, it is essential to reconsider the disciplinary boundary between International Relations and Conflict Resolution. These two disciplines should stimulate each other by sharing analytical concepts and theories. For example, the concept of "deterrence", which is deeply rooted in International Relations with a focus on nuclear deterrence and superpower confrontation, is rarely introduced in Conflict Resolution, particularly in the context of disciplinary discussions about the role of international peacekeepers or intervention forces. However, because many armed conflicts have both international and intra-state elements, it is crucial to overcome these disciplinary barriers and perception biases to achieve a more comprehensive understanding.

2.4 Political Realism and the State-Centric Bias

The state-centric bias in the discipline of International Relations has its roots in the early years of its establishment. Hans Morgenthau played a pivotal role in shaping this bias with the publication of his book, *Politics among Nations*, in 1948. Morgenthau strongly criticized what he referred to as idealism during the inter-war period. (Morgenthau, 1946, 1948).

After World War I, the study of international affairs tended to emphasize the necessity for institutional reforms within international systems. Advocates of this perspective, particularly prevalent in the United States, often supported the idea of strong international organizations. Morgenthau, however, took issue with this idealist approach. He believed that the efforts to outlaw war initiated by US President Woodrow Wilson after World War I were part of an idealist campaign and, in Morgenthau's view, were misguided. He argued that wars would persist because powerful states would not relinquish their pursuit of power in international politics. According to Morgenthau, international politics is defined as an arena where states engage in a continuous struggle for power while pursuing their national interests.

The foundational concept in International Relations, according to Morgenthau, is that states are powerful entities destined to engage in wars. This perspective influenced the discipline's focus on international wars rather than conflicts within states. Throughout the Cold War period, International Relations remained centered on the rivalry between superpowers in the twentieth century and European great power politics up to the nineteenth century.

Even with the emergence of new theories such as "neo-realism" (structural realism) by Kenneth Waltz (Waltz, 1979), "hegemonic stability" by Charles Kindleberger, Robert Gilpin, and Stephen Krasner, and "offensive realism" by John Mearsheimer (Mearsheimer, 1990: 5–56), the state-centric nature of International Relations theories persisted. These theories continued to focus on great power confrontations and prioritize the actions and interactions of sovereign states, maintaining the state-centric bias that had been established in the discipline's early years.

The state-centric bias in International Relations persisted after the end of the Cold War. Scholars within the discipline turned their attention to the transformation of the international order from the Cold War era to the post-Cold War period. The twentieth-century international order was often described as the creation of hegemonic US power, a concept prominent in discourses such as the "Liberal International Order" proposed by John Ikenberry (Ikenberry, 2001). It was anticipated that the post-Cold War international order would follow a similar trajectory, with the relations among great powers determining the structure of international society.

During this period, little attention was directed toward small-scale intra-state conflicts outside the sphere of influential great powers in the discipline of International Relations. The prevailing narrative shifted with the emergence of the myth of the "victory of liberal democracy" as an expression of the "soft power" of the United States and the other Western powers (Fukuyama, 1992). The theory of the "democratic peace," advocated by scholars like Bruce Russett, propagated the idea that the ideological hegemony of the West, based on liberal democratic values, was continuously consolidating (Russet, 1993).

As the decline of US power became evident and the assumed ideological supremacy of the West diminished, however, the recent circumstances were characterized as a "return of geopolitics" (Mead, 2014) against the backdrop of the "liberal international order" (Ikenberry, 2014). Critics of the US-led international order emphasized the "tragedy of great power politics" (Mearsheimer, 2014) positing that great power rivalry remained a major structural determinant of international society. This critical perspective challenged the notion that liberal democracy and the dominance of Western values were the primary driving forces shaping the international order, bringing attention back to the enduring dynamics of power politics among states.

2.5 Theories of Conflict Resolution and the Myth of New Wars

During the Cold War period, Conflict Resolution theories did not necessarily assume that contemporary armed conflicts were exclusively intra-state. The emergence of Peace Studies, pioneered by Johan Galtung and featuring concepts such as "negative and positive peace," was not primarily focused on distinguishing between international wars and intra-state armed conflicts (Galtung, 2004). Instead, the development of Conflict Resolution theories during this time documented efforts to find analytical tools for prescriptive practices, particularly in response to the ideological standpoints derived from general political theories.

Peace Studies, as introduced by Johan Galtung, aimed to explore and understand the root causes of conflicts and to develop strategies for achieving both negative peace (the absence of war) and positive peace (the absence of structural violence such as injustice and inequality). This perspective did not limit itself to a specific type of conflict but sought to address a broad range of conflicts, whether international or intra-state.

The development of Conflict Resolution theories during the Cold War era was driven by a desire to move beyond ideological stances and contribute practical insights to resolving conflicts. Scholars in this field worked on refining analytical tools that could be applied to various conflicts, irrespective of their international or intra-state nature. The focus was on offering practical and prescriptive solutions to the complexities of conflicts rather than adhering to rigid distinctions between different types of conflicts.

John Burton's contributions to Conflict Resolution include the development of the "human needs theory" and the "problem-solving" approach (Burton, 1990). The human needs theory focuses on addressing the root causes of conflicts by fulfilling the basic needs of individuals and communities. This approach aims at preventing aggression and promoting peace. The "problem-solving" method involves analyzing the parties involved in a conflict, bringing them to the negotiation table to discuss their relationships, working towards establishing agreements that acknowledge the problems and their associated costs, and exploring possible options for resolution. Burton's theories did not require a strict distinction between international wars and intra-state armed conflicts (Burton, 1972).

Edward Azar's theory of "protracted social conflict" delves into the structural causes of conflicts, particularly those within communal groups. Azar identified basic needs, including security, recognition, acceptance, fair access to political institutions, and economic participation, as fundamental elements in understanding and addressing conflicts. These needs are categorized into security, development, political access, and identity needs. While Azar's framework can be applied to analyze the structures of intra-state armed conflicts, it does not necessarily focus exclusively on them (Azar, 1990).

In summary, both Burton and Azar contributed to Conflict Resolution by providing frameworks that emphasize addressing the root causes of conflicts and promoting dialogue and negotiation. These approaches are applicable to a wide range of conflicts, whether they are international or intra-state in nature. The theories highlight the importance of understanding and addressing the basic needs of individuals and communities to achieve sustainable peace.

A significant shift occurred with the emergence of the myth of "new wars" in contrast to "old wars," marking a symbolic sea change (Kaldor, 2001). The prevailing assumption suggested that while old-type international wars characterized the period before the end of the Cold War, the post-Cold War era witnessed a rise in intra-state armed conflicts. However, this generalization was largely false. The hypothesis superficially gained momentum with the general perception of a changing era immediately after the end of the Cold War.

This shift in perspective led to the popularization of the "liberal peacebuilding theory," which faced criticism for its perceived ideological bias (Paris, 2004). The assumption of liberal peacebuilding theory is that the establishment of a liberal democracy is not only ideologically desirable but also politically stable. Liberal democracy was understood to be a tool to establish durable peace in domestic society after an intra-state conflict. This assumption was not rigidly tested; rather dubious, but believed in the environment of the era after the "victory of liberal democracy" (Richmond, 2011). As a result, a dichotomy emerged: while International Relations continued to focus on the study of international wars in history and theory, Conflict Resolution became the discipline that primarily analyzed intra-state armed conflicts as ongoing contemporary issues. This division reflected a broader trend in academic discourse, where the changing nature of conflicts and the evolving global landscape influenced how scholars approached and studied conflicts. The emphasis on intra-state armed conflicts in Conflict Resolution highlighted the complexities and challenges associated with conflicts within sovereign states, moving away from the traditional focus on international wars that had characterized much of the Cold War era.

William Zartman is renowned for his contributions to the field of Conflict Resolution, particularly for introducing concepts such as "ripeness" and "mutually hurting stalemate (MHS)" (Zartman, 2003). He stated, "As the dominant system of conflict and world order disintegrates, internal conflicts and their regional ramifications emerge as the primary challenge to international peace and security." (Zartman, 2019: 161) This viewpoint is shared by other major theoreticians on conflict causes, including scholars like Paul Collier and Francis Stewart. While their perspectives may not be exclusively constrained by the distinction between international wars and intra-state armed conflicts, their analyses often delve into the conditions prevalent in domestic societies. For instance, scholars like Collier and Stewart have explored the causal factors of armed conflict, considering conditions such as the dependence of national revenues on natural resources and social inequality among sub-national groups within a state (Collier, 2000a, b, pp. 91–111) (Stewart, 2008). Their work underscores the idea that addressing internal dynamics and conditions within a society is crucial for understanding and effectively resolving armed conflicts. This shift in focus toward internal conflicts reflects the changing nature of global conflicts, with scholars recognizing that conflicts within states can have significant regional and international implications. The emphasis on internal dynamics and root causes aligns with a more comprehensive approach to conflict resolution that considers the complexities of domestic societies in addressing the challenges to international peace and security.

In this context, Russia's full-scale invasion of Ukraine in 2022 shocked many researchers who felt unprepared to deal with major international wars as subjects of conflict analysis. However, the armed conflict involving Russian troops had already been underway in Ukraine's eastern part well before 2022, known as the Donbas War since 2014. In reality, Ukraine has been at war with Russia since 2014, punctuated by temporary nominal ceasefires such as the Minsk Agreements. The Donbas War was not terminated by the 2022 full-scale invasion; rather, it evolved. Given that the major battlefields of the Russo-Ukrainian War were in the eastern part of the country, especially from 2023 onward, it appears that the Donbas War continues to be merged with the larger international conflict known as the Russo-Ukrainian War.

The intermingling of intra-state armed conflict and international war in Ukraine is not exceptional, as seen in other cases like Syria, Yemen, Somalia, Ethiopia, Democratic Republic of Congo, and other countries. These circumstances underscore the urgent need to remove the disciplinary constraint of demarcating between "intra-state conflict" and "international war". Instead, there is a strong need to integrate insights from Conflict Resolution and International Relations to better understand and analyze the reality of "international intra-state wars".

2.6 Reflections on the Constraints of Policy Perspectives in Conflict Resolution

The limitations of academic perspectives in Conflict Resolution and International Relations, particularly the relative lack of integrated theories to analyze "international intra-state armed conflicts," may mirror the challenges faced in implementing conflict resolution measures in practice. International Relations often sheds light on "deterrence" among great powers, exemplified by nuclear deterrence between nuclear-armed nations. However, it rarely addresses contemporary armed conflicts as arenas where the perspective of "deterrence" can be applied. Practitioners seldom discuss "deterrence" in the context of resolving armed conflicts in practice. During the Cold War, the United Nations developed monitoring activities through UN peacekeeping operations between multiple state conflict parties in the Middle East, Cyprus, Kashmir, and other regions. However, there was hesitancy to intervene in the domestic spheres of sovereign states to conduct monitoring actions between actors within the same sovereign state.

Unlike during the Cold War, conflict resolution measures after the Cold War emphasized interventions in the domestic spheres of sovereign states. For instance, when NATO launched military interventions in Bosnia and Herzegovina and Kosovo, and when ECOWAS intervened in Liberia and Sierra Leone in the 1990s, there was a clear perception that these interventions occurred within the domestic spheres of sovereign states. These actions were conducted as "enforcement" under the banner of collective security, driven by the understanding that conflict resolution measures might need to take the form of intervention when the governments of sovereign states are part of the conflict problem, and resolution cannot solely rely on those governments. The frequent use of the authority of Chapter VII of the UN Charter by the UN Security Council underscores this trend. With or without military interventions for "enforcement," international actors provide assistance in the form of development aid, framed as "peace-building" or even "state-building" efforts in domestic jurisdictions. These efforts often include governance reforms in state apparatuses, such as security sector reforms, judicial reforms, reforms in legal frameworks, and capacity development programs. The underlying assumption is that conflicts arise because the state lacks the capacity to govern society or the willingness to comply with internationally standardized norms, presupposing that contemporary armed conflicts are predominantly intra-state conflicts.

2.7 Reality of Armed Conflicts in the Contemporary World

As discussed earlier, the problematic presupposition underlying policy assumptions becomes evident with the increasing number of armed conflicts, giving rise to the phenomenon of "international intra-state armed conflicts." Contrary to the general observation emerging in the 1990s that armed conflicts primarily result from state fragility and poor governance, the widespread occurrence of international intra-state armed conflicts challenges the assumption that intra-state factors are the major causes of such conflicts. Several patterns in the international arena shed light on the factors influencing contemporary armed conflicts.

The first pattern pertains to the impact of the end of the Cold War, marked by the collapse of the Soviet Union and its communist regime. The periphery of Russia, comprising former USSR republics that gained independence from the Russian Federation, became a notable conflict-prone area in the contemporary world. From Ukraine and Moldova (Transnistria) in Europe, through South Ossetia and Abkhazia in Georgia, Nagorno-Karabakh in Azerbaijan, Chechnya in Russia within the wider Caucasus region, to Tajikistan and other volatile areas in Central Asia, the periphery of the former USSR is replete with records of armed conflicts in the post-Cold War period. The pattern of Russia's military intervention is a prevalent feature, underscoring the international dimension inherent in these conflicts.

The second pattern is observed in the significant impact of the Global War on Terror. While the broader concept of combating terrorism dates back to the twentieth century, the so-called Global War on Terror commenced with the US invasion of Afghanistan in 2001 to remove Al-Qaeda and the Taliban regime following the 9/11 attacks in New York and Washington, D.C. The 2003 "Iraq War" resulted in disastrous consequences for the country, the region, and for the US and its allies. The Arab Spring, armed conflicts in the Middle East and North Africa (MENA), and the rise of the Islamic State (IS) further fueled terrorist activities, extending to the Horn of Africa and the Sahel region in Africa. Many of these groups pledged allegiance to either IS or Al-Qaeda, establishing connections with their networks. The Global War on Terror expanded from South Asia through the Middle East to Africa.

The third pattern arises from the fragility that invites international interventions. After the Arab Spring, numerous authoritarian regimes faced challenges from anti-government movements, leading to varying responses. Some regimes brutally suppressed these movements with international support, as seen in Syria, while others descended into factional wars with foreign intervenors, exemplified by Libya. Coup d'états unfolded in the Sahel, accompanied by internationally instigated disinformation, misinformation, and the presence of foreign mercenaries.

The legitimacy of liberal democracy is globally contested, as evidenced by incidents of violence during elections even in the United States, where groups like the Proud Boys operate actively. With the waning political and economic power of the West, traditional democracies face accusations of a double standard, particularly in their disparate approaches to conflicts in Ukraine and Gaza. When universal applicability is compromised, skepticism about liberal democracies, driven by perceptions of hypocrisy, becomes inevitable.

2.8 Conflict Resolution Policies Need to Be Adjusted

The era of ambitious agendas for peacebuilding and state-building has passed. Few donors can afford to sustain large investments for extensive projects aimed at renewing sovereign states. UN peacekeeping operations continue to see downsizing in their budgets, personnel, size, and operational scope (United Nations, 2024). Even humanitarian aid activities began to be downsized in 2023 (United Nations, 2023). Given this challenging reality, conflict resolution policies must be adjusted realistically to align with the conditions on the ground.

Firstly, the traditional measure of "deterrence" should be discussed in conflict resolution, responding to many international intra-state armed conflicts in the contemporary world. With the weakening and loosening of US power after the rapid expansion of NATO, partner states are urged to increase their defense efforts. In line with this process, (sub-)regional organizations such as the EU, AU, and ECOWAS have emerged as security providers. While they have clear limits in their operational capacities, they are expected to function as deterrence mechanisms by compensating for the lack of strong military alliances to deter instability in their regions. This applies to countries like Ukraine, which aspires to accede to NATO but may not be able to do so in the near future. There must be some kind of deterrence system to prevent the spread and re-occurrence of armed conflicts once they are alleviated or terminated. The package of so-called "security guarantees" is supposed to be a deterrence system through weapon provisions, capacity development, information sharing, and other measures.

Secondly, the traditional measure of "monitoring" should be reassessed in the context of the downsizing of peacekeeping operations and the reluctance to conduct military interventions as "enforcement" actions. Methods of UN peacekeeping operations are becoming outdated. The pretense of a universal organization may continue to be undermined by the Security Council, as it fails to decide on important policy agendas due to serious confrontations among the permanent members. The effectiveness of economic sanctions is being seriously questioned. In the end, elaborate manners of mediation for peace through negotiation must be patiently respected, with careful introductions of ad-hoc monitoring mechanisms and the way they operate in gradation of areas. In short, more modest approaches to conflict resolution need to be revalued, with reinforced investments in the areas of mediation and monitoring. In the case of large countries such as Ukraine, universal nationwide implementation of monitoring is practically impossible. Therefore, there should be ad-hoc mechanisms of monitoring in gradation systems, which could classify the national territory into different areas.

Thirdly, the recent approach to peacebuilding, particularly regarding ambitious reform agendas, needs to be scaled back. The diminishing credibility of liberal democracy negatively affects the way peacebuilding agendas are pursued. With reduced funding for peacebuilding projects, it is crucial to prioritize conflict resolution efforts. The Hobbesian concentration of power in the central government may not work effectively under circumstances where universal values are seriously questioned. More gradual, nuanced, and locally-owned approaches to peacebuilding need to be mainstreamed. In addition, regional settings beyond national borders are indispensable. In the case of Ukraine, which is becoming a strong military power in the region, assurances of confidence-building measures with neighboring countries must be pursued through an informal platform for dialogue among regional partners. Multi-layered conflict management systems with multiple partners would be necessary (Shinoda, 2024).

2.9 Concluding Remarks

The theory and practice of conflict resolution need revitalization to better address the challenges of our changing and complex world. This chapter has contended that unless the theory and practice of conflict resolution adapt more effectively to the phenomenon of "international intra-state armed conflicts", the bias towards the dominance of intra-state armed conflicts in the contemporary world will persist. A combined approach that draws on the theoretical insights of both Conflict Resolution and International Relations is necessary to overcome this bias. Implementing domestic reforms and promoting international partnerships in a combined manner is also essential to tackle the increasing number of international intra-state armed conflicts.

The relevance of the Free and Open Indo-Pacific (FOIP) is underscored in this context. While FOIP itself is not a conflict resolution mechanism, the partnerships envisioned by the Free and Open Indo-Pacific should be strengthened and leveraged for conflict resolution purposes. Partnerships for conflict resolution can be formed within the framework of FOIP, and existing forums like the Tokyo International Conference on African Development (TICAD) could be enhanced within the FOIP framework by expanding the number of sponsoring states. For example, Japan does not have to host TICAD alone and may rather position it as a forum to broaden its partnership with other FOIP-committed countries.

Take Ukraine as an example, as it is relevant to FOIP. Ukraine maintains the status of a maritime power, and the Indo-Pacific area is connected to the Black Sea through the Red Sea and the Mediterranean Sea. The management of free and open seas is crucial for FOIP partners. The vision of FOIP as a platform for partnership in maintaining free and open seas should be visibly pursued for the purpose of conflict resolution as well.

References

Azar, E. E. (1990). *The management of protracted social conflict: Theory and cases.* Dartmouth Pub Co.
Burton, J. W. (1972). Resolution of conflict. *International Studies Quarterly, 16*(1).
Burton, J. (1990). *Conflict: Resolution and provention.* St Martin's Press.
Collier, P. (2000a). Doing well out of war: An economic perspective. In M. Berdal, & D. M. Malone (Eds.), *Greed and grievance: Economic agendas in civil wars.* Lynne Rienner Publishers.
Collier, P. (2000b). *Greed and grievance in civil war.* Policy Research Working Paper 2355. World Bank.
Davies, S., Engström, G., Pettersson, T., & Öberg, M. (2024). Organized violence 1989–2023, and the prevalence of organized crime groups. *Journal of Peace Research, 61*(4), 673–693.
Fukuyama, F. (1992). *The end of history and the last man.* Free Press.
Galtung, J. (2004). *Transcend and transform: An introduction to conflict work.* Pluto Press.
Ikenberry, G. J. (2001). *After victory: Institutions, strategic restraint, and the rebuilding of order after major wars.* Princeton University Press.
Ikenberry, G. J. (2014). The illusion of geopolitics: The enduring power of the liberal order. *Foreign Affairs, 93*(3).
Kaldor, M. (2001). *New and old wars: Organized violence in a global era.* Stanford: Stanford University Press.
Mead, W. R. (2014). The return of geopolitics: The revenge of the revisionist powers. *Foreign Affairs, 93*(3).
Mearsheimer, J. (1990). Back to the future: Instability in Europe after the Cold War. *International Security, 15*(1).
Mearsheimer, J. (2014). *Tragedy of great power politics.* W W Norton & Co Inc.
Morgenthau, H. (1946). *Scientific man versus power politics.* University of Chicago Press.
Morgenthau, H. (1948). *Politics among nations: The struggle for power and peace.* Knopf.
Pairs, R. (2004). *At war's end: Building peace after civil conflict.* Cambridge University Press.
Richmond, O. (2011). *A post-liberal peace.* Routledge.
Russet, B. (1993). *Grasping the democratic peace: Principles for a post-Cold War world.* Princeton Univ Press.
Shinoda, H. (2024). *Partnership peace operations: UN and regional organizations in multiple layers of international security.* Routledge.
Stewart, F. (2001). *Horizontal inequalities: A neglected dimension of development.* Working Paper 1: Centre for Research on Inequality, Human Security and Ethnicity, CRISE Queen Elizabeth House, University of Oxford.
Stewart, F. (2008). *Horizontal inequalities and conflict: Understanding group violence in multi-ethnic societies.* Palgrave Macmillan.
UCDP (Uppsala Conflict Data Program). (2023). *State-based conflicts by type of conflict (1946–2023).* https://ucdp.uu.se/downloads/charts/
United Nations. (2023). *Global humanitarian overview 2024.* United Nations.
United Nations. (2024). *Fifth committee approves $5.59 billion budget for 14 peacekeeping operations, service centres, headquarters support staff, concluding resumed session.* https://press.un.org/en/2024/gaab4463.doc.htm. Accessed October 27, 2024.
Waltz, K. (1979). *Theory of international politics.* McGraw-Hill.

Zartman, W. (2003). Understanding ripeness: Making and using hurting stalemate. In R. Mac Ginty, & A. W. -S. John (Eds.), *Contemporary peacemaking: Peace processes, peacebuilding and conflict*. Palgrave Macmillan.

Zartman, W. (2019). Chapter 9: Dynamics and constraints in negotiating internal conflicts. In *I William Zartman: A pioneer in conflict management and area studies: Essays on contention and governance*. Springer.

Open Access This chapter is licensed under the terms of the Creative Commons Attribution-NonCommercial-NoDerivatives 4.0 International License (http://creativecommons.org/licenses/by-nc-nd/4.0/), which permits any noncommercial use, sharing, distribution and reproduction in any medium or format, as long as you give appropriate credit to the original author(s) and the source, provide a link to the Creative Commons license and indicate if you modified the licensed material. You do not have permission under this license to share adapted material derived from this chapter or parts of it.

The images or other third party material in this chapter are included in the chapter's Creative Commons license, unless indicated otherwise in a credit line to the material. If material is not included in the chapter's Creative Commons license and your intended use is not permitted by statutory regulation or exceeds the permitted use, you will need to obtain permission directly from the copyright holder.

Chapter 3
The International Implications of the Russo-Ukrainian War

Iurii Perga

Contents

3.1	Unity, Tensions, and Divisions in Europe: The So-Called "Return of Geopolitics"	28
	3.1.1 The Unity of the West	28
	3.1.2 The Tensions and Divisions Within the West	29
	3.1.3 The Return of Geopolitics	30
3.2	Fragility and Vulnerability in Africa	30
	3.2.1 The Impact of the War on the Environment and Economics	31
	3.2.2 The Impact of the War on Food Security in West Africa	31
	3.2.3 The Impact of the War on Political Stability in West Africa	32
	3.2.4 The Wagner Group Case	32
	3.2.5 Russian Soft Power in Africa	33
	3.2.6 Chinese Economic Influence in Africa	33
3.3	Ambiguity in the Middle East and Asia: The Impact of the Russo-Ukrainian War	34
	3.3.1 The Impact of the War on Food Security	34
	3.3.2 The Impact of the War on Political Stability	35
	3.3.3 The Impact of the War on Regional Security Arrangements	36
	3.3.4 The Impact of the War on the Security Dynamics of East Asia	36
	3.3.5 The Impact of the War on Economic Relations Between East Asia and Russia	37
	3.3.6 The Impact of the War on the Political Alignment of East Asian Countries	38
	3.3.7 The Impact of the War on Domestic Politics in East Asia	38
3.4	Summary Conclusion	39
	References	40

Abstract The Russo-Ukrainian War, initially viewed as a European conflict, has generated far-reaching impacts across regions like the Middle East and South Asia. Though geographically distant, these areas have been significantly affected by disruptions in global supply chains, energy markets, and political alignments. With the war interrupting the supply of vital commodities such as wheat, corn, and sunflower oil, countries in these regions—notably Yemen, Lebanon, and Egypt—have faced soaring food prices, heightening food insecurity, and economic challenges. Already grappling with domestic issues, these nations have become increasingly vulnerable

---

I. Perga (✉)
Igor Sikorsky Kyiv Polytechnic Institute, Kyiv, Ukraine
e-mail: y.perga@kpi.ua

to the war's indirect impacts. This chapter examines how the conflict has reshaped economic, political, and security dynamics in the Middle East and Asia, highlighting the interconnected nature of today's global landscape. Through food, energy, and security dependencies, the ripple effects of the Russo-Ukraine conflict reveal that no region remains untouched, underscoring the far-reaching implications of modern warfare. A separate chapter addresses the implications for North America and NATO. This allows a focused analysis of how the Russo-Ukrainian War impacts these regions specifically.

Keywords Russo-Ukrainian war · Food security · Supply chains · Economic instability · Geopolitical dynamics · Energy dependence · Political vulnerability

3.1 Unity, Tensions, and Divisions in Europe: The So-Called "Return of Geopolitics"[1]

While the West has collectively reinforced support for Ukraine through sanctions, military aid, and political solidarity, key divisions remain, particularly regarding relations with China and energy dependencies. The war has also underscored the return of geopolitics, with NATO expansion, heightened defense spending, and strategic shifts in Europe's approach to Russia. This evolving landscape challenges Western cohesion and global partnerships.

3.1.1 The Unity of the West

The war between Russia and Ukraine has dramatically reinforced the solidarity of Western nations, highlighting a solid collective response in support of Ukraine. This unity has manifested in shared economic sanctions against Russia, extensive financial and military support, and a firm stance across international platforms like the G7, NATO, and the European Union (EU). For instance, since 2022, the EU and the United States have implemented multiple sanctions targeting critical sectors of the Russian economy, including oil, technology exports, and the financial system, aiming to weaken Russia's war capabilities (European Council, 2022a, b). Military aid to Ukraine has been substantial, with the United States providing over $40 billion in military assistance by 2023, including advanced weaponry like HIMARS, which

---

[1] The phrase 'return of geopolitics' is often employed in analyses of shifting global power dynamics, as discussed by Walter Russell Mead in *"The Return of Geopolitics: The Revenge of the Revisionist Powers"* and countered by John Ikenberry in *"The Illusion of Geopolitics: The Enduring Power of the Liberal Order"* (Foreign Affairs, May/June 2014). Mead argues that revisionist powers seek to reshape the current order, whereas Ikenberry suggests the liberal order retains resilience despite these challenges.

played a pivotal role in Ukraine's defense (United States Department of Defense, 2023).

In 2023, discussions around Ukraine's future EU and NATO membership have intensified. At the NATO Vilnius summit in July 2023, Ukraine's potential accession was once again reaffirmed, signaling that NATO views Ukraine as a critical part of its future security architecture (NATO, 2023). This support has been further bolstered by the European Union's accelerated political and economic integration with Ukraine. The EU granted Ukraine candidate status for membership in 2022, marking a significant political shift amid the ongoing war. Such unity and shared policy actions demonstrate the strategic alignment of Western nations, especially in the context of deterring Russia's ambitions.

3.1.2 The Tensions and Divisions Within the West

However, this unity is not without its challenges. The war has exacerbated underlying tensions and divergences within the Western alliance, especially concerning the level and nature of military and economic support for Ukraine. A clear example of this division is the hesitation of some countries, like Hungary, which has consistently voiced objections to certain EU sanctions on Russia. Hungary's Prime Minister, Viktor Orbán, has maintained economic ties with Moscow, criticizing energy sanctions that disproportionately affect Hungary due to its heavy reliance on Russian gas. This divergence was evident in early 2023, when Hungary delayed EU plans to impose a new round of sanctions, highlighting fissures within the EU (Politico, 2023).

Additionally, the broader strategic relationship with China has created tension within the West. French President Emmanuel Macron's visit to China in April 2023, alongside German Chancellor Olaf Scholz's earlier diplomatic engagements, underscores European nations' differing approaches toward Beijing. While the United States seeks to rally its European allies to take a tougher stance on China, particularly regarding economic decoupling and technology restrictions, some EU nations prefer maintaining open channels of dialogue and trade. This was notably reflected in the divergent responses to China's peace proposal for Ukraine in February 2023, which France and Germany viewed cautiously, while others, like the U.S., dismissed it as a superficial diplomatic maneuver (Gabuev, 2023).

Economic dependencies have also been a sticking point. In 2022, Montenegro's debt to China for infrastructure projects underscored how economic entanglements could complicate the geopolitical posture of smaller European states. Moreover, Germany's 2023 negotiations to allow a Chinese company a stake in Hamburg's port infrastructure sparked debates over the risks of Chinese investment in strategic assets (Radio Free Europe/Radio Liberty, 2023). These examples illustrate how differing national interests, strategic dependencies, and views on global partnerships create fault lines within the Western alliance, particularly with China.

3.1.3 The Return of Geopolitics

The conflict has led to what some have termed the "return of geopolitics" in Europe, with a renewed focus on territorial security and power competition. This shift is evident in the European Union's prioritization of defense spending, NATO's expansion, and reassessing relations with Russia. The NATO Strategic Concept adopted in 2022 marked a significant turning point, refocusing the alliance's efforts on deterring Russian aggression and expanding military capabilities along its eastern flank. This includes the deployment of additional NATO troops to countries like Poland, the Baltic states, and Romania to reinforce collective defense. NATO's increased budget allocation in 2023, bolstered by commitments from member states to increase their defense spending to 2% of GDP, further reflects this shift (Atlantic Council, 2024).

This return to a geopolitically charged atmosphere is also visible in the recalibration of European foreign policy toward Russia. The 2022 and 2023 energy crises, exacerbated by Russia's weaponization of gas supplies, forced Europe to pivot away from its reliance on Russian energy hastily. The EU's REPowerEU plan, launched in 2022, aimed at reducing energy dependence on Russia by 2030, has accelerated the transition toward renewable energy sources and diversified gas supplies, including increased imports of liquefied natural gas (LNG) from the United States and Qatar (European Commission, 2024).

As of 2024, Europe's political and strategic landscape remains deeply influenced by the war. The European Union continues to grapple with the challenge of presenting a unified front on foreign policy matters. The EU's role in brokering peace deals or influencing the outcome of the war remains limited by its internal divisions and its complex relationship with global powers like China and the U.S. This reemergence of geopolitics also poses a long-term challenge for the EU, as it must navigate the delicate balance between supporting Ukraine and managing its strategic interests globally.

3.2 Fragility and Vulnerability in Africa

The Russo-Ukrainian War has accentuated the fragility and vulnerability of African nations across multiple dimensions, notably in environmental, economic, and political stability areas. Africa's position in the global economy, heavily reliant on energy and food imports, makes it especially susceptible to the ripple effects of international conflicts. This is further compounded by the region's pre-existing challenges, including climate change, political instability, and slow recovery from the COVID-19 pandemic.

3.2.1 The Impact of the War on the Environment and Economics

The war has profoundly affected global energy markets, leading to sharp increases in oil and gas prices. As a result, African countries, particularly in East Africa, increasingly turn to more ecologically damaging energy sources to meet their demands (Reuters, 2022a, b, c, d, e, f). For instance, Kenya and Tanzania have seen a resurgence of coal usage, which had declined before the war, as the price of oil and gas soared in 2022 and 2023. This pivot to coal and other non-renewable energy sources threatens to exacerbate environmental degradation and deforestation in already vulnerable areas. Kenya's energy ministry noted a 20% increase in coal consumption in the second half of 2023, marking a significant setback for its renewable energy goals (National Treasury of Kenya, 2024).

The economic fallout from the war has similarly created ripple effects across Africa, particularly for economies still recovering from the COVID-19 pandemic. Inflation rates surged across the continent in 2022 and 2023 due to rising fuel prices, pushing millions back into poverty (International Monetary Fund, 2022a, b). Countries such as Ethiopia and Uganda, which rely heavily on imported fuel, witnessed inflation soar to over 30% by mid-2023, mainly driven by energy costs and supply chain disruptions. The International Monetary Fund (IMF) reported that Africa's economic growth was expected to slow to 3.7% in 2023, down from the pre-war projection of 4.5% (International Monetary Fund, 2023). This economic slowdown further strains fragile economies already grappling with high levels of debt and unemployment.

3.2.2 The Impact of the War on Food Security in West Africa

One of the most visible impacts of the war has been on food security, particularly in West Africa, which is heavily dependent on grain imports from Russia and Ukraine (Food and Agriculture Organization, 2023). The war has disrupted these vital supply chains, sharply increasing regional food prices. This price shock is particularly devastating for countries already facing food insecurity due to climate change and ongoing conflicts. For example, in Niger, the cost of wheat had risen by 40% by mid-2022, exacerbating an already precarious food security situation. By early 2023, more than 20% of Niger's population was classified as food insecure, further stretching the country's limited resources (Food and Agriculture Organization, 2023).

In Mali, the war disrupted the flow of food aid to displaced populations, leading to increased malnutrition rates. According to the World Food Programme (WFP), more than 4 million people in Mali needed food assistance by the end of 2022, with children being the most affected. The WFP had to revise its distribution schedules several times due to supply disruptions caused by the war (World Food Programme, 2022a, b).

Nigeria, Africa's largest economy, was also hit hard by the war's impact on agricultural inputs, particularly fertilizers. Nigeria is a significant importer of fertilizers from Russia, and the disruption in supply led to a 30% drop in availability by mid-2022 (CGIAR, 2022). This, in turn, reduced crop yields in the 2023 growing season, contributing to a surge in food prices. By the end of 2023, staple food prices such as maize and sorghum had risen by over 50%, prompting widespread concerns about food affordability, particularly for lower-income households (Nigerian National Bureau of Statistics, 2022).

3.2.3 The Impact of the War on Political Stability in West Africa

The war in Ukraine has not only disrupted food and energy markets but has also transformed the security landscape in West Africa. The region has become more vulnerable to political instability, terrorism, and economic disruptions, creating a new layer of fragility. A series of military coups in 2022 and 2023 in countries like Burkina Faso, Guinea, and Niger underscored the deepening instability across the region. These coups were partly driven by disillusionment with governments' inability to tackle the worsening security and economic conditions exacerbated by the war's global fallout.

The Economic Community of West African States (ECOWAS) has struggled to respond to these crises effectively (Al Jazeera, 2022a, b). In Niger, a military coup in 2023 led to the ousting of President Mohamed Bazoum, further weakening the regional stability. This event raised concerns over the future of democratic governance in West Africa as military juntas consolidated power in several countries. Meanwhile, jihadist movements, such as those linked to al-Qaeda and the Islamic State, have exploited the power vacuum and rising discontent in the region, launching attacks in Mali, Burkina Faso, and Nigeria (United Nations, 2022a, b).

The disintegration of regional security structures has been worsened by the proliferation of weapons flowing from conflict zones, including those originating from Russian arms sales. By 2024, the United Nations reported a significant increase in illicit arms transfers into the Sahel region, further destabilizing a volatile area. This influx of weapons has not only fueled local conflicts. Still, it has also strengthened terrorist groups that operate across national borders, contributing to the growing fragility of West Africa's security landscape (United Nations, 2022a, 2022b).

3.2.4 The Wagner Group Case

The Russian private military company Wagner Group has played an increasingly visible role in Africa, aligning with Russia's geopolitical objectives. The group has been implicated in military and security operations in countries such as Libya, Sudan, and the Central African Republic (CAR), where its activities have often aligned with securing natural resources and countering Western influence. For example, Wagner's presence in CAR has been instrumental in bolstering the government's military capabilities against rebel groups while also securing mining rights for Russian companies (Geneva Centre for Security Policy, 2024).

After the death of Wagner's leader, Yevgeny Prigozhin, in 2023, the group will likely be integrated into the formal structures of the Russian military or intelligence services. This development could strengthen Russia's influence across Africa, allowing Moscow to deepen its geopolitical foothold in strategically important regions such as North and Central Africa. Wagner has been instrumental in securing strategic locations such as oil fields and military bases in Libya, effectively expanding Russia's leverage in North African geopolitics.

3.2.5 Russian Soft Power in Africa

Russia's approach to Africa extends beyond military involvement and includes a sophisticated soft power strategy. This multifaceted approach leverages media, religious institutions, and cultural diplomacy to expand Russian influence across the continent. Russia Today (RT), a state-funded international television network, has been critical in shaping African public opinion, particularly by offering narratives that challenge Western perspectives on global events. RT has gained traction in African nations like South Africa, Nigeria, and Kenya, where its alternative news coverage resonates with audiences disillusioned with Western media outlets (Texty.org.ua, 2023).

The Russian Orthodox Church has also been active in Africa, working closely with Russian diplomatic and cultural missions. Through promoting Orthodox Christianity, the Church serves as a vehicle for spreading Russian cultural and ethical values (Jamestown Foundation, 2023). This religious outreach has been particularly evident in countries like Ethiopia and Kenya, where Orthodox Christianity already has a historical presence. The Church's activities complement Russia's broader efforts to cultivate cultural and religious ties with African nations, enhancing its soft power on the continent.

3.2.6 Chinese Economic Influence in Africa

China's economic influence in Africa has become one of the most significant geopolitical developments in recent years. The Belt and Road Initiative (BRI) is central to China's engagement with Africa, providing a framework for infrastructure development that connects African countries to global trade networks (Army University

Press, 2023). Since 2022, China has invested heavily in transport and energy infrastructure in East Africa, with major projects such as the Mombasa-Nairobi railway in Kenya and the Addis Ababa-Djibouti rail link in Ethiopia.

However, China's economic engagement with Africa has not been without controversy. The issue of "debt diplomacy" has come under increased scrutiny as several African countries struggle to repay the large loans provided by China for infrastructure projects. In 2023, Zambia became the first African nation to default on Chinese loans, leading to concerns that other countries could face similar debt crises (Reuters, 2023a, b). By 2024, countries like Angola and Kenya were facing mounting pressure to renegotiate their debt terms with China, raising alarms about the sustainability of these financial arrangements.

Critics argue that these large-scale loans, while enabling infrastructure development, lead to unsustainable debt levels, effectively increasing African countries' economic dependency on China. This has sparked debates within African governments about the long-term implications of such economic ties, with some countries, like Tanzania, opting to scale back on specific BRI projects to avoid falling into a debt trap. At the same time, China's investments have undeniably contributed to the economic modernization of parts of Africa, creating jobs and improving trade connectivity (Economist, 2024).

3.3 Ambiguity in the Middle East and Asia: The Impact of the Russo-Ukrainian War

The ongoing war in Ukraine has had profound effects far beyond Europe, with significant repercussions in the Middle East and South Asia. These regions have felt the impact through disruptions in food security, political instability, the rise of non-state actors, and shifting security dynamics. As importers of food, energy, and resources from Russia and Ukraine, these regions are particularly vulnerable to the consequences of the war.

3.3.1 The Impact of the War on Food Security

The war in Ukraine has severely disrupted global food supply chains, particularly affecting the Middle East and South Asia, where many nations depend highly on food imports from Ukraine and Russia (Food and Agriculture Organization, 2022a, b). Ukraine is a major global exporter of wheat, corn, and sunflower oil, and the war has prevented these commodities from reaching their usual markets. The resultant shortages have driven food prices, exacerbating already fragile economies in these regions (World Bank, 2022).

One of the most severe cases is Yemen, where a combination of war, economic collapse, and dependency on food imports has led to a humanitarian crisis. Yemen imports approximately 45% of its wheat from Ukraine and Russia, and the disruption of this supply has significantly worsened food shortages. By mid-2022, the United Nations reported that 19 million people in Yemen were facing acute food insecurity, with children particularly vulnerable to malnutrition. Rising food prices, driven by the war, have made it increasingly difficult for many in Yemen to access basic foodstuffs (World Food Programme, 2022a, b).

In Lebanon, the war has compounded the country's severe economic crisis. Lebanon imports around 80% of its wheat from Ukraine, and the supply disruptions have led to food prices surging (Al Jazeera, 2022a, b). By 2023, the bread cost in Lebanon had doubled, further stressing a population already grappling with hyperinflation and unemployment. The United Nations warned in 2023 that Lebanon faced an imminent risk of famine unless alternative food supplies could be secured (United Nations, 2023).

Similarly, Egypt, one of the world's largest wheat importers, has faced food security challenges due to the war. Egypt sources nearly 85% of its wheat from Russia and Ukraine (Reuters, 2022a, b, c, d, e, f). By early 2023, wheat prices had risen by over 50%, forcing the Egyptian government to introduce bread subsidies to prevent mass food insecurity. The country has also struggled to find alternative grain sources, driving up inflation and exacerbating social unrest.

3.3.2 The Impact of the War on Political Stability

The political ramifications of the war have extended into the Middle East and South Asia, contributing to a broader destabilization of the global order. The war has heightened concerns about these regions' political and economic stability and the potential for increased tensions between neighboring states.

The war has exacerbated tensions between the government and the opposition in Egypt. As food prices and inflation rose in 2022 and 2023, the Egyptian government faced growing discontent from the public and political opposition. The opposition has accused the government of being too aligned with Western interests, particularly the United States, while the government has charged the opposition with sympathizing with Russia. This domestic friction is part of a broader trend of increased polarization in Egyptian politics (Al-Monitor, 2022).

In South Asia, the war has further strained relations between India and Pakistan, two nuclear-armed neighbors with a long history of conflict. Both countries have found themselves caught in the broader geopolitical ramifications of the war. India's neutral stance on the war and its continued purchases of Russian oil have drawn criticism from the West. At the same time, Pakistan's historically close ties to China and the United States have complicated its position (Reuters, 2022a, b, c, d, e, f). Concerns exist that the war could exacerbate tensions between the two countries, particularly as both seek to navigate shifting alliances.

In Lebanon, the war has worsened the country's internal political divisions. The country's dependence on food imports and an already collapsed economy have heightened social unrest and created opportunities for political factions to exploit the situation for their gains. Hezbollah, which has ties to both Iran and Russia, has used the war to strengthen its political influence in Lebanon, further destabilizing the country's fragile political environment (Polska Akademia Nauk, 2022).

3.3.3 The Impact of the War on Regional Security Arrangements

The war in Ukraine has raised serious questions about the effectiveness of regional security arrangements in the Middle East and South Asia. These arrangements, such as the Gulf Cooperation Council (GCC) and the South Asian Association for Regional Cooperation (SAARC), were designed to promote stability and deter conflict. However, the war has exposed its limitations, particularly in preventing major powers from engaging in aggressive actions.

The GCC, which includes Saudi Arabia, Kuwait, the United Arab Emirates, Qatar, Bahrain, and Oman, has condemned Russia's invasion of Ukraine but has not taken any concrete steps to deter further aggression (Reuters, 2022a, b, c, d, e, f). This is partly due to the GCC's complex relations with Russia and the West. Russia's influence in the region, particularly in Syria, and its role in global oil markets make it a key player that the GCC countries cannot antagonize (Atlantic Council, 2022a, b). By 2023, the GCC's response remained largely symbolic, underscoring the difficulty of balancing diplomatic relations with competing global powers (United States Government Publishing Office, 2022).

Similarly, SAARC, which includes India, Pakistan, Bangladesh, Nepal, Bhutan, Sri Lanka, and the Maldives, has also been largely ineffective in addressing the geopolitical fallout of the war (The Diplomat, 2022a, b). While SAARC member states have expressed solidarity with Ukraine, the organization has not played a significant role in mitigating the broader effects of the conflict. This reflects the broader limitations of regional organizations in managing global crises that have far-reaching economic and political implications.

3.3.4 The Impact of the War on the Security Dynamics of East Asia

The war in Ukraine has also raised concerns about security dynamics in East Asia, particularly for countries that share borders with Russia and China. The war has prompted several countries to reassess their defense policies and alliances in response to the changing global security landscape.

Japan, in particular, has significantly increased its defense spending in response to the war. In April 2022, Japan announced that it would double its defense budget from 1 to 2% of GDP, marking a historic shift in its post-World War II pacifist stance (Nikkei Asia, 2023). The acquisition of new weapons systems, including missile defense technology, accompanied increased military spending. By 2023, Japan had conducted several joint military exercises with the United States and regional partners such as South Korea and Australia to counterbalance China's growing regional influence (Reuters, 2023a, b).

South Korea has also taken steps to strengthen its military capabilities. In May 2022, South Korea deployed an additional THAAD missile defense system designed to intercept ballistic missiles amid growing concerns about North Korea's nuclear ambitions and the broader security implications of the war in Ukraine (The Diplomat, 2022a, b). By 2024, South Korea had deepened its military alliance with the United States, conducting joint naval drills with Japan and the U.S. in the East China Sea (Reuters, 2024). These actions highlight the growing security coordination among U.S. allies in the region.

The AUKUS security pact, which involves the United States, the United Kingdom, and Australia, has also intensified security activities in the region. During 2022 and 2023, the three countries increased their military cooperation, conducting naval drills and enhancing their military presence in the Indo-Pacific (The Guardian, 2022). This reflects the broader geopolitical shift triggered by the war in Ukraine, as nations in East Asia seek to bolster their defenses against potential threats from both Russia and China.

3.3.5 The Impact of the War on Economic Relations Between East Asia and Russia

The economic fallout from the war has disrupted relations between East Asia and Russia. Many countries in East Asia, particularly Japan and South Korea, have imposed sanctions on Russia in response to its invasion of Ukraine (Reuters, 2022a, b, c, d, e, f). These sanctions have included bans on oil imports and restrictions on financial transactions, which have harmed the Russian economy and East Asian businesses with ties to Russia.

In March 2022, Japan announced that it would ban the import of Russian oil, marking a significant break from its previous energy (The Japan Times, 2022). Similar sanctions from the United States, the European Union, and other countries followed this move. The sanctions have severely affected Russia's oil exports, which constitute a primary source of revenue for the country. By 2023, Russia had lost significant market share in East Asia, with countries like Japan and South Korea turning to alternative energy suppliers.

The economic impact of the war has also been felt across the broader East Asian region. In May 2022, the Asian Development Bank (ADB) downgraded its economic growth forecast for the area, citing the war's effects on energy prices and global trade. The ADB warned that the war could lead to prolonged inflation and slower economic growth, particularly for countries reliant on imports of Russian energy and commodities (Asian Development Bank, 2022).

3.3.6 The Impact of the War on the Political Alignment of East Asian Countries

The war has had a significant impact on the political alignment of countries in East Asia. Japan and South Korea have aligned more closely with the United States in response to the conflict, while other countries, such as Vietnam, have sought to maintain a more neutral stance.

In March 2022, Japan and South Korea joined the United States in imposing sanctions on Russia, marking a significant shift in their foreign policy. Japan had previously avoided taking a strong stance against Russia due to its energy dependency. However, the war has prompted Japan and South Korea to reevaluate their geopolitical priorities, leading to a closer alignment with U.S. policies on Russia and China.

In contrast, Vietnam has taken a more cautious approach. In May 2022, Vietnam announced it would not join the United States and its allies in imposing sanctions on Russia. This decision reflects Vietnam's desire to balance its relations with the United States and Russia and its broader strategy of maintaining neutrality in global conflicts. By 2023, Vietnam had continued to pursue a policy of non-alignment while still engaging in diplomatic dialogue with both Western and Russian officials.

3.3.7 The Impact of the War on Domestic Politics in East Asia

The war in Ukraine has also had domestic political consequences for countries in East Asia. In Japan, the war has led to increased support for the ruling Liberal Democratic Party (LDP), as the government's firm stance against Russia has been well-received by the public (Reuters, 2022a, b, c, d, e, f). By 2023, Prime Minister Fumio Kishida had consolidated his political position, with opinion polls showing increased public approval of his foreign policy.

In South Korea, however, the war has led to increased criticism of the government's handling of the North Korean nuclear threat. The opposition has accused President Yoon Suk-yeol of being too soft on North Korea, arguing that the war in Ukraine demonstrates the dangers of not taking a firm stance against potential aggressors. This criticism has fueled political tensions in South Korea, with debates over defense spending and foreign policy dominating the national discourse.

In China, the war has led to increased censorship and suppression of dissent. The Chinese government has sought to control the narrative surrounding the war, with state media presenting a carefully curated image of neutrality. However, reports of growing anti-war sentiment among the Chinese public, particularly on social media platforms, have emerged. By 2024, the Chinese government had intensified its efforts to suppress dissent, reflecting its concerns about the potential for domestic unrest triggered by the war's broader geopolitical implications (United States-China Economic & Security Review Commission, 2024).

3.4 Summary Conclusion

The Russo-Ukrainian War has acted as a seismic event in the geopolitical landscape, altering the power dynamics within Europe and exposing significant cracks in the global order. The conflict has brought old problems to the surface, such as food insecurity, energy dependencies, and regional instability, while simultaneously giving rise to new powers and alliances that challenge the traditional dominance of Western nations. This war, far from being an isolated European issue, has had far-reaching consequences, reshaping international relations and exacerbating vulnerabilities in regions as diverse as the Middle East, Africa, South Asia, and East Asia.

The war has exposed the fragility of the current global system. Long-standing institutions such as the United Nations, the Gulf Cooperation Council (GCC), and the South Asian Association for Regional Cooperation (SAARC) have struggled to address the complex challenges posed by the conflict, illustrating their limitations in preventing and mitigating large-scale global crises. The failure of these organizations to offer concrete solutions to the war's consequences, from food insecurity to political instability, underscores the need to reassess their roles in a rapidly evolving world order.

Old problems thought to be under control have resurfaced with renewed intensity. Food insecurity, particularly in vulnerable regions like West Africa, the Middle East, and South Asia, has become a pressing global issue. The war has disrupted vital supply chains, causing food prices to skyrocket, which in turn has exacerbated economic inequality and political unrest. Similarly, the energy crisis triggered by the war has forced nations to revert to environmentally harmful practices, undermining global efforts to combat climate change.

At the same time, the war has accelerated the rise of new powers and alliances that challenge the hegemony of traditional Western-dominated institutions. Russia, despite facing economic sanctions and military setbacks, continues to expand its influence in regions like Africa and the Middle East, using both hard and soft power tactics. The Wagner Group, for instance, has played a pivotal role in securing Russia's geopolitical interests in Africa, aligning itself with local governments and exploiting regional instability. Similarly, China's growing influence, mainly through its Belt and Road Initiative, has positioned it as a critical player in reshaping the economic and political landscape of regions heavily affected by the war's fallout.

In this evolving geopolitical context, non-Western coalitions like BRICS are gaining prominence. Their increasing influence in global governance signifies a shift in the balance of power as developing nations seek alternatives to the traditional Western-led world order. This realignment of global alliances reflects the broader cracks in the international system as nations are forced to adapt to the changing dynamics of power, influence, and security.

The Russo-Ukrainian War has, in essence, catalyzed a realignment of global power structures, revealing both the fragility of the current world order and the emergence of new actors on the international stage. As old problems reemerge and new powers rise, the world finds itself at a critical juncture, where the existing system must either evolve to meet these challenges or face further fragmentation and instability.

References

Al Jazeera. (2022, August 12). *Lebanon news update*. https://www.aljazeera.com/news/2022/8/12/lebanon

Al Jazeera. (2022, February 3). *ECOWAS emergency summit on coups in West Africa*. https://www.aljazeera.com/news/2022/2/3/ecowas-emergency-summit-coups-west-africa

Al-Monitor. (2022, March). *Egypt's balancing act between the US and Russia amid Ukraine war*. https://www.al-monitor.com/originals/2022/03/egypt-seeks-middle-ground-between-us-russia-ukraine-fighting-rages

Army University Press. (2023). *China's belt and road initiative*. https://www.armyupress.army.mil/Journals/Military-Review/English-Edition-Archives/May-June-2023/Chinas-Belt/

Asian Development Bank. (2022). *Outlook April 2022*. https://www.adb.org/outlook/editions/april-2022

Atlantic Council. (2022). *The Ukraine war and Saudi Arabia's relations with the US and China*. https://www.atlanticcouncil.org/blogs/menasource/the-ukraine-war-is-making-saudi-arabia-and-the-uae-rethink-how-they-deal-with-us-pressure-over-china/

Atlantic Council. (2024). *NATO-Russia dynamics: Prospects for reconstitution of Russian military power*. https://www.atlanticcouncil.org/in-depth-research-reports/report/nato-russia-dynamics-prospects-for-reconstitution-of-russian-military-power/

CGIAR. (2022). *Climate change and armed groups*. https://cgspace.cgiar.org/server/api/core/bitstreams/2d1a8012-a5c2-4e14-bbfa-7625381981f0/content

Economist. (2024, September 4). *China's murkier relations with Africa*. https://www.economist.com/middle-east-and-africa/2024/09/04/chinas-relationship-with-africa-is-growing-murkier

European Commission. (2024). *REPowerEU: Affordable, secure, and sustainable energy for Europe*. https://commission.europa.eu/strategy-and-policy/priorities-2019-2024/european-green-deal/repowereu-affordable-secure-and-sustainable-energy-europe_en

European Council. (2022). *Council Decision (EU) 2022/265 of 28 February 2022 concerning restrictive measures in response to the Russian aggression against Ukraine*. https://eur-lex.europa.eu/legal-content/EN/TXT/PDF/?uri=CELEX:32022D0335

Food and Agriculture Organization. (2022a). *Food Security and Nutrition 2022 report*. https://openknowledge.fao.org/server/api/core/bitstreams/3d62caef-1749-404e-8217-6ac4783a135b/content

Food and Agriculture Organization. (2022b). *State of food security and nutrition in the world: 2022*. https://openknowledge.fao.org/server/api/core/bitstreams/bd0267ca-75a6-44d6-a387-7ebeb150630d/content

Food and Agriculture Organization. (2023c). *The state of food security and nutrition in the world*. https://www.fao.org/publications/home/fao-flagship-publications/the-state-of-food-security-and-nutrition-in-the-world/2023/en

Gabuev, A. (2023, March). *Inside China's peace plan for Ukraine*. Carnegie Endowment for International Peace. https://carnegieendowment.org/russia-eurasia/politika/2023/03/inside-chinas-peace-plan-for-ukraine?lang=en

Geneva Centre for Security Policy. (2024). *Geneva Paper No. 32*. https://dam.gcsp.ch/files/doc/geneva-paper-32-2024

International Monetary Fund. (2022a, April). *Regional economic outlook for sub-Saharan Africa*. https://www.imf.org/en/Publications/REO/SSA/Issues/2022/04/28/regional-economic-outlook-for-sub-saharan-africa-april-2022

International Monetary Fund. (2022b, April). *World Economic Outlook database*. https://www.imf.org/en/Publications/WEO/weo-database/2022/April

International Monetary Fund. (2023). Regional economic outlook: Sub-Saharan Africa, April 2023. Retrieved from https://www.imf.org/en/Publications/REO/SSA/Issues/2023/04/14/regional-economic-outlook-for-sub-saharanafrica-april-2023.

Jamestown Foundation. (2023). *Moscow Patriarchate moves into Africa, aiding Kremlin and disturbing Orthodox unity*. https://jamestown.org/program/moscow-patriarchate-moves-into-africa-helping-kremlin-but-roiling-orthodox-world/

NATO. (2023). *Vilnius Summit Communiqué*. https://www.nato.int/cps/en/natohq/216570.htm

National Treasury of Kenya. (2024). *Kenya Power 2022/2023 report*. https://www.treasury.go.ke/wp-content/uploads/2024/05/Kenya-Power-2022_2023.pdf

Nigerian National Bureau of Statistics. (2022). *Consumer price index report, December 2022*. https://www.nigerianstat.gov.ng/pdfuploads/CPI%20DECEMBER%202022%20REPORT.pdf

Nikkei Asia. (2023). *Japan to increase defense budget to 2% of GDP by 2027*. https://asia.nikkei.com/Politics/Japan-set-to-increase-defense-budget-to-2-of-GDP-in-2027

Politico. (2023). *Ukraine warns Russian ally Hungary to stop blocking EU sanctions*. https://www.politico.eu/article/ukraine-warns-russian-ally-hungary-to-stop-blocking-eu-sanctions/

Polska Akademia Nauk. (2022). *Research articles on international relations*. https://bibliotekanauki.pl/articles/24020099

Radio Free Europe/Radio Liberty. (2023). *Hungary EU sanctions list: Russia, Ukraine*. https://www.rferl.org/a/hungary-eu-sanctions-list-russia-ukraine/32227730.html

Reuters. (2022a, December). *Egypt's wheat imports decrease, with increased reliance on Russian wheat*. https://www.reuters.com/article/markets/currencies/egypt-relied-on-competitive-russian-wheat-as-imports-dipped-in-2022-data-idUSKBN2TR0ZI/

Reuters. (2022b, July 10). *Japan's ruling coalition maintains majority in upper house elections*. https://www.reuters.com/world/asia-pacific/view-japan-ruling-coalition-seen-keeping-majority-upper-house-2022-07-10/

Reuters. (2022c, March 1). *Japan freezes Russian central bank assets as part of new sanctions*. https://www.reuters.com/world/europe/japan-freezes-assets-russias-central-bank-part-new-sanctions-2022-03-01/

Reuters. (2022d, March 16). *Saudi Arabia's strategic dilemma with Russia and China*. https://www.reuters.com/world/saudi-prince-rebuked-by-west-faces-dilemma-over-russia-china-2022-03-16/

Reuters. (2022e, March 19). *India's oil imports from Russia increase amid criticism*. https://www.reuters.com/business/energy/indias-oil-imports-us-rise-amid-criticism-russian-purchases-2022-03-19/

Reuters. (2022f, October 4). *African countries push common energy position at COP27*. https://www.reuters.com/world/africa/african-countries-push-common-energy-position-cop27-2022-10-04/

Reuters. (2023, April 15). *US, Japan, and South Korea hold missile defense exercises*. https://www.reuters.com/world/asia-pacific/us-japan-south-korea-hold-missile-defence-exercises-deter-north-korea-threat-2023-04-15/

Reuters. (2023, September 19). *Chinese loans to Africa drop to near two-decade low*. https://www.reuters.com/world/africa/chinese-loans-africa-plummet-near-two-decade-low-study-2023-09-19/

Reuters. (2024, April 12). *South Korea, Japan, and US naval drills amid North Korea threats*. https://www.reuters.com/world/asia-pacific/south-korea-japan-us-hold-naval-drills-amid-nkorea-threats-2024-04-12/

Texty.org.ua. (2023). *How Russian Orthodox Church spreads Russian narratives in Africa*. https://texty.org.ua/articles/113299/how-russian-orthodox-church-spreads-russian-narratives-africa/

The Diplomat. (2022, March). *Asian countries' votes on the UN's Ukraine resolution*. https://thediplomat.com/2022/03/how-did-asian-countries-vote-on-the-uns-ukraine-resolution/

The Diplomat. (2022, October). *South Korea's THAAD upgrade issues*. https://thediplomat.com/2022/10/the-trouble-with-south-koreas-thaad-upgrade/

The Guardian. (2022, April 5). *AUKUS pact expands to include hypersonic weapons development*. https://www.theguardian.com/politics/2022/apr/05/aukus-pact-extended-to-development-of-hypersonic-weapons

The Japan Times. (2022, May 9). *Japan's participation in Russian oil project Sakhalin*. https://www.japantimes.co.jp/news/2022/05/09/national/japan-russisan-oil-sakhalin/

United Nations. (2022). *Climate change and armed groups report*. https://peacekeeping.un.org/sites/default/files/climate_change_and_armed_groups_full_report.pdf

United Nations. (2022). *Document archive*. https://digitallibrary.un.org/record/3999468?v=pdf

United Nations. (2023). *Lebanon crisis response plan 2023*. https://lebanon.un.org/sites/default/files/2023-05/Lebanon%20Crisis%20Response%20Plan%202023_0.pdf

United States Department of Defense. (2023). *Ukraine security assistance*. https://www.defense.gov/News/News-Stories/Article/Article/3854245/dod-announces-additional-security-assistance-for-ukraine/

United States Government Publishing Office. (2022). *China's stance on Russia's invasion of Ukraine*. https://sgp.fas.org/crs/mideast/R47160.pdf

United States-China Economic and Security Review Commission. (2024). *China's position on Russia's invasion of Ukraine*. https://www.uscc.gov/research/chinas-position-russias-invasion-ukraine

World Bank. (2022). *Food security update, July 29*. https://thedocs.worldbank.org/en/doc/40ebbf38f5a6b68bfc11e5273e1405d4-0090012022/original/Food-Security-Update-LXVII-July-29-2022.pdf

World Food Programme. (2022). *Ukraine conflict: Addressing acute needs, protecting displaced populations*. https://www.wfp.org/publications/april-2022-ukraine-conflict-addressing-acute-needs-protecting-displaced-populations

World Food Programme. (2022). *Yemen Situation Report*. https://www.ecoi.net/en/file/local/2077106/2022+03+WFP+Yemen+External+Situation+Report+March+%281%29.pdf

Open Access This chapter is licensed under the terms of the Creative Commons Attribution-NonCommercial-NoDerivatives 4.0 International License (http://creativecommons.org/licenses/by-nc-nd/4.0/), which permits any noncommercial use, sharing, distribution and reproduction in any medium or format, as long as you give appropriate credit to the original author(s) and the source, provide a link to the Creative Commons license and indicate if you modified the licensed material. You do not have permission under this license to share adapted material derived from this chapter or parts of it.

The images or other third party material in this chapter are included in the chapter's Creative Commons license, unless indicated otherwise in a credit line to the material. If material is not included in the chapter's Creative Commons license and your intended use is not permitted by statutory regulation or exceeds the permitted use, you will need to obtain permission directly from the copyright holder.

Chapter 4
The Impact of the Russo-Ukrainian War on NATO: Implications for the Strategic Concept of the Alliance

Tomonori Yoshizaki and Hideaki Shinoda

Contents

4.1	Introduction	44
4.2	Emergence of "Ukrainian Dilemma"	44
	4.2.1 Hybrid Warfare	45
4.3	NATO's Preparedness for Hybrid Warfare	46
4.4	Alliance "Missions": Strengthening Ukraine's Resilience and Deterring and Defending Against Russia	46
	4.4.1 The Task of Supporting Ukraine: Strengthening Resilience	47
	4.4.2 The Alliance's "Extended Deterrence" and Ukraine	49
	4.4.3 Operations Not Assigned by NATO	50
4.5	The Alliance's "Capabilities"	51
	4.5.1 The NRF's "Deterrence and Defense" Mission	52
4.6	The Alliance's "Division of Labor"	53
4.7	Implications for Japan-NATO Cooperation Across the Indo-Pacific Region	55
References		56

Abstract Russia's full-scale invasion of Ukraine shocked the member states of the NATO (North Atlantic Treaty Organization) and led to the reconsideration of its Strategic Concept as regards "mission", "capacity", and "role-share". In 2014 NATO started facing the "Ukrainian Dilemma" through the "hybrid warfare". Since then, NATO has been struggling to support Ukraine without directly confronting Russia. This is a fundamental challenge to the concept of the alliance. There are critical implications in the efforts of NATO for the future of Japan and the Free and Open Indo-Pacific (FOIP).

Keywords NATO (North Atlantic Treaty Organization) · EU (European Union) · Russia's full-scale invasion of Ukraine · Strategic concept · Ukrainian dilemma · Hybrid warfare · Japan · Free and open Indo-Pacific (FOIP)

T. Yoshizaki · H. Shinoda (✉)
Tokyo University of Foreign Studies, Tokyo, Japan
e-mail: hshinoda@tufs.ac.jp

T. Yoshizaki
e-mail: tomoyoshizaki@tufs.ac.jp

4.1 Introduction

This chapter explores the impact of the Russo-Ukrainian War upon NATO. While Ukraine is not a member state, NATO has been heavily committed to the defense of Ukraine. Why? How? What will be the role of the alliance in this new configuration? These are the question this essay addresses. Russia's invasion of Ukraine has fundamentally changed NATO's Strategic Concept, which will be analyzed here from three perspectives: mission, capabilities, and division of labor.

The first is the extent to which the alliance can pursue a common "mission". Member states on the North American continent across the Atlantic and in Europe have different geopolitical conditions and diverse perceptions of national interests and national strengths. In addition, after the Cold War, NATO has been actively involved in conflicts outside the region, using force in the former Yugoslavia and Afghanistan, and has even been responsible for supporting state reconstruction. And now the question of the extent to which it should be tasked with providing assistance to neighboring partner country Ukraine, which is not a member, has emerged.

Secondly, does the alliance have the "capacity" to carry out its mandate? Traditionally, the Alliance has been a form of security cooperation based on protecting the sovereignty and territorial integrity of member states. However, as NATO's missions expand and change globally, the question is whether the alliance is prepared to have the military capabilities to meet these changes.

Third, how to "role-share" the alliance's required missions and capabilities among its members: the "annexation" of Crimea in 2014 was the catalyst for NATO to call for stronger deterrence and defense against Russia, and set a numerical target of 2% of defense spending as a percentage of gross domestic product (GDP). It remains to be seen whether Russia's recent invasion of Ukraine will further strengthen the joint defense orientation and increase pressure for role-sharing by member states. This essay analyses NATO's response to the Russo-Ukrainian War from the above three perspectives.

4.2 Emergence of "Ukrainian Dilemma"

Russia's full-scale invasion of Ukraine has transformed the international strategic environment, and the impact of the crisis on the US-EU alliance is extremely complex. On the one hand, Ukraine is not a NATO member but a partner country. As such, Ukraine is not subject to direct defense or extended deterrence by NATO. On the other hand, Ukraine is located at a strategic juncture and any threat to its independence or sovereignty would have a major impact on the surrounding region. The country borders Russia to the east, Poland, Slovakia and Hungary to the west, Romania and Moldova to the south and Belarus to the north. NATO cannot therefore overlook aggression against its partner country, Ukraine. In addition, the civilian casualties caused by President Vladimir Putin's "special military operations" have been condemned by the international community as a humanitarian crisis.

NATO cannot be responsible for the direct defense of Ukraine, but neither can it sit by and watch Russia's invasion of Ukraine. And it cannot send the wrong signal that NATO is weak-kneed as Putin readies Russia's nuclear posture. NATO faces a "Ukrainian dilemma", as international political scientist Janice Gross Stein has put it.

For NATO, this complex composition was created by Russia's "annexation" of the Crimean peninsula in 2014. In this section, we will look back at the 2014 crisis and see how NATO has changed as an alliance to pursue different roles, capabilities, and role-sharing.

4.2.1 Hybrid Warfare

From December 2021 onwards, the signs of Russia's invasion of Ukraine were clearly visible, and the day of a military invasion by Russia, the so-called "X-Day", was reported in the media due to the large amount of information disclosed by the US. At the time, there was also a strong prospect that the "Hybrid Warfare" approach of annexing the Crimean Peninsula, starting in February 2014, would be taken again, however. For this reason, this section looks back at Russia's hybrid warfare approach in its annexation of Crimea in 2014, followed by how NATO strengthened its readiness to respond to this. In terms of results, Russia went far beyond the hybrid warfare framework when it launched a full-scale invasion of northern, eastern and southern Ukraine on 24 February 2022. However, it is also true that the preparations for forward defense since the 2014 crisis have provided for Russian preparations for an invasion of Ukraine. It is with these issues in mind that this chapter revisits the 2014 crisis.

From February 2014 onwards, Russia began military exercises under the guise of "unannounced inspections". It moved into the Crimean peninsula and eastern regions of Ukraine to establish itself and annexed Crimea through a referendum. This approach, later called hybrid warfare, was followed by special military operations in which armed forces, presumed to be Russian special forces, suppressed strongholds such as airports and broadcasting stations. After these military operations, Russian troops moved into Ukraine to "protect" the Russian population and "guard" Russian military bases, ending the exercise. Subsequently, the Crimean parliament, which hads a majority of Russian descent, voted to secede from Ukraine (Freedman, 2014: 7–38; and McDermott et al., 2014).

4.3 NATO's Preparedness for Hybrid Warfare

Traditional deterrence is less effective against Russian hybrid warfare, where the lines between military and non-military are blurred. NATO was therefore called upon to work seamlessly with the European community to prepare for Russian hybrid warfare. Thus, NATO returned to deterrence and defense in Europe: since the attacks of 2001, NATO has been busy with the "long war" in Afghanistan and Iraq. However, following Russia's unilateral change of status quo in the Crimean Peninsula, NATO was forced to completely rethink its strategy. At its core was a reaffirmation of the alliance's joint defense mission (the so-called Article V mission).

Since 2014, NATO's "return to Europe" has moved quickly. US President Barack Obama made the following speech in the Estonian capital Tallinn in September of the same year. The defense of Tallinn, Riga and Vilnius is as important as the defense of Berlin, Paris and London. By Article 5 of the Treaty it is clear that an attack on one country is an attack on the whole. The differences between the Baltic states and Britain, France and Germany are obvious, but the alliance's obligation of collective defense puts the member states in the same league. This emphasis on the unity of the alliance and reassurance to the citizens of member states is called reassurance and was the axis of Obama's support for NATO. This reassurance is the counterpart to deterrence, the concept of preventing attacks on allies. The Donald Trump administration then moved beyond Obama's trust provision to put military deterrence at the forefront, but the basic policy remained the same (Deni, 2017).

Russia's hybrid war in 2014 appeared to be an unexpected surprise for NATO. However, NATO countries, which had long experienced stability operations in distant Afghanistan and were skilled in civil-military coordination with the local population and NGOs (CIMIC), did not fail to respond to hybrid warfare. From this point onwards, new missions and capabilities will be developed, including a response to Russian hybrid warfare.

4.4 Alliance "Missions": Strengthening Ukraine's Resilience and Deterring and Defending Against Russia

A report published in 2017 by the International Institute for Strategic Studies (IISS) in London described the crises in Ukrain as "the mudslinging in Eurasia after the collapse of the Soviet Union". Policies there can only have negative consequences and "everyone is a loser". Russia claims "protection" of the Russian population in the Donbas region of eastern Ukraine through the secession of the "Donetsk People's Republic" and the "Lugansk People's Republic". The conflict was prolonged as the western powers-imposed sanctions against Russia, appealing to the international community over the tragedy of the Crimean Peninsula's deprivation of some two million inhabitants. Thus, in February 2022, the war would open (Charap and Colton, 2017: 151).

NATO's mission in the face of the Russian invasion of Ukraine can be considered on two levels. The first is the level of support to Ukraine under attack by Russian forces. This corresponds to the crisis management mission as an alliance. The second is the level of strategic posture to deter attacks against NATO members. This corresponds to the deterrence and defense mission as an alliance. These two aspects will be discussed in terms of how NATO has defined its own mission in order to stop its military provocations against Russia, which has committed acts of aggression, and to impose maximum costs on Moscow.

4.4.1 The Task of Supporting Ukraine: Strengthening Resilience

How to support the sovereignty and independence of the Alliance's partner country Ukraine without risking a direct confrontation with Russia? A measure to mitigate this "Ukraine Dilemma" is to strengthen the resilience of NATO member states: it does not have a mandate to directly defend its partner country Ukraine, nor can it be expected to be capable of defending the Donbass region, which lies further out than NATO's eastern wing. The shortcut to minimizing the aftermath of the Russo-Ukrainian War is therefore to strengthen the resilience of NATO member states themselves. This logic has the universality of improving national governance, and therefore it is a logic that encourages and, if necessary, supports the "self-help" of neighboring partner countries and Ukraine.

The Resilience Principles were adopted by NATO at the Warsaw Summit in 2016, with an emphasis on "national and collective resilience and civilian readiness" in advancing the response to the hybrid war after 2014 (NATO, 2016). Its treaty provision is Article 3, which states that "States Parties, singly and jointly, shall maintain and develop their individual and collective capacity to resist armed attack by means of continuous and effective self-help and mutual assistance".

Regarding the Russo-Ukrainian War, the urgency for neighboring partner state Ukraine, which borders NATO member states, to continue to maintain its own sovereignty and territorial integrity, was synonymous with increasing national resilience.

When focusing on the resilience of sovereign states, the international consequences of the fall of Kabul, Afghanistan, on 15 August 2021 cannot be ignored. About six months before Russia's full-scale invasion of Ukraine, Afghanistan, which NATO had been helping to rebuild the state for almost two decades, fell into the hands of the Taliban. The country's president, Ashraf Ghani, had secretly left the country with his property. Having lost their head of state, the Afghan military and police surrendered the capital to the Taliban without resistance, and resilience disappeared. The US "long war" came to an unexpected end.

About six months later, on 24 February 2022, Putin launched a military invasion, but Ukraine never followed the Afghanistan rut. Led by President Volodymyr

Zelensky, the Ukrainian Government put forward an all-out defensive stance and appealed to the rest of the world for immediate support through the digital technologies of web conferencing and social networking. The actions taken by the Ukrainian Government were in compliance with the seven key NATO-led resilience principles, as seen below.

First, the continuation of government functions. This was symbolized by President Zelensky's call for immediate assistance to defend the capital city of Kyiv via the web and the world's media: he took part in the NATO Council of Foreign Ministers communicating his intention to resist Russia.

Second, the resilience of energy supplies. Since the beginning of the war, Russia has continued its attacks on power plants, including a nuclear power plant in the north of Kyiv, and has occupied parts of it. However, Ukraine's domestic energy supply is backed up from abroad and the electricity grid is maintained.

Third, it is dealing with the large number of refugees and displaced persons. According to the Office of the United Nations High Commissioner for Human Rights (UNHCR), there were approximately 5.6 million Ukrainian refugees in the period from the Russian military invasion to 2 May, 2022. Poland was the largest refugee destination with over 3 million people, followed by Romania, Russia, Hungary, Moldova, Slovakia, and Belarus. In the context of a serious and protracted humanitarian crisis, NATO is accelerating troop deployment and equipment supply to Member States bordering Ukraine.

Fourth, it is ensuring the supply of food and water resources. The rapid increase in the number of refugees and displaced persons mentioned above has increased the importance of NATO's Civil-Military Cooperation (CIMIC) support to Ukraine.

Fifth, in order to cope with mass casualty outbreaks, the civilian medical health system should be made functional on a regular basis, and sufficient medicines and equipment should be prepared and secured. This also requires collaboration and cooperation with international organizations and international NGOs. A report by the humanitarian NGO Human Rights Watch describing the devastation in the city of Bucha, north-west of Kyiv, adds that it "preserves evidence that is essential for the prosecution of war crimes". In European politics, these humanitarian crises raise highly sensitive issues.

Sixth, the resilience of civilian communications systems. The need to maintain and operate information and communication networks and provide the necessary back-up, even during ongoing crises, is also key to the Zelensky Government's strategic communication.

And seventh, a resilient transport system, which requires NATO forces to move quickly within the Alliance's territory and to ensure a transport network envisaged for both civilian and military use. This perspective is in line with the EU's emphasis on Military Mobility.

Thus, in the face of a full-scale invasion by Russian forces, Ukraine sought support through action in line with the resilience principle. Kyiv's approach to communicating globally through the new domain of cyberspace can be described as being in line with NATO's push for strategic communication.

4.4.2 The Alliance's "Extended Deterrence" and Ukraine

Alliances are built around pledges of mutual security cooperation between member states, and NATO is no exception: the North Atlantic Treaty (Washington Treaty), signed in 1949, has collective defense at its core. NATO Secretary General Jens Stoltenberg has repeatedly referred to Article 5 during the Russo-Ukrainian War.

NATO's stated military mission is threefold: "deterrence, defense and combat". Unexpectedly, the Russian invasion of Ukraine has put these alliance missions to the test. Let us examine each of them below.

At the beginning of the war, the Russian military launched an invasion of eastern, southern, and northern Ukraine, and touted "war results", such as declaring itself in control of the airspace, giving the impression that NATO's extended deterrence was ineffective. However, to date, the fighting has been confined to Ukraine and no direct Russian armed attacks have occurred against the 32 NATO member states.

There have been no direct armed attacks against member states in the Baltic Sea region and the north-east wing of NATO, including Poland, where NATO has launched a forward defense since the Crimean crisis in 2014, nor in the south-east wing of NATO, including the Black Sea region. In other words, NATO's extended deterrence can be described as functioning. In a new development, Sweden and Finland, which have traditionally advocated a policy of neutrality, have now changed their stance to apply for NATO membership. This can be assessed as a growing expectation of NATO's ability to deter enlargement.

Nevertheless, general deterrence on the European continent is facing a test as the crisis in Ukraine, which borders NATO member states, escalates and becomes more protracted. So what moves is NATO making to ensure the credibility of extended deterrence to its allies? At present, this mainly manifests itself in the form of security cooperation, including the activation of the NATO Defense Plan and the deployment of the Readiness Force (NRF), as well as the transfer of equipment to Ukraine.

First, in the face of the emergency situation of Russia's invasion of Ukraine, NATO launched its first Defense Plan. Following this, the NATO Readiness Force (NRF) was for the first time made operational with a "deterrence and defense" mission—the NRF was created in 2004 at the initiative of Defense Secretary Rumsfeld in the US Bush (son) administration. It was also expected to serve as an intervention force (spearhead force) as the Global War on Terror intensified. However, its actual operational performance has been limited to relatively minor crisis management missions in extra-territorial operations. For example, the NRF mainly monitored the presidential election in Afghanistan and provided assistance to disaster-affected areas after natural disasters such as the Pakistan earthquake and hurricanes in the US. The reason the NRF did not operate as an intervention force is said to be that France and other European countries wanted to give priority to the EU in developing a rapid response force. The crisis of 2014 changed this trend, and now the NRF is operational with a deterrence and defense mission.

The second Ukrainian equipment transfer supports the country's resilience in military terms. NATO members, led by the US and UK, actively supplied portable, short-range equipment, including Javelin anti-tank missiles and Stinger air defense missiles. These were provided to the Ukrainian side for use in base defense, helping to halt the advance of the Russian land forces and offset air superiority by the air force.

In addition to this, there have been moves from Central and Eastern European countries that were members of the former Warsaw Pact Organization to provide Ukraine with equipment such as tanks made in the former Soviet Union. Ironically, equipment transfers are still relatively easy because they were part of the same military alliance during the Cold War. To cite just one example, Poland has approached Ukraine about providing MIG-29 and SU-27 fighters and T-72 tanks, the Czech Republic about T-72 tanks, and Slovakia about providing S-300 air defense systems to Ukraine. Such former Soviet equipment does not meet NATO standards and is therefore almost never used by NATO members in former Central and Eastern Europe, even if stored. It paves the way for Ukraine possession of Bundeswehr's Leopard-II tanks, thereafter.

How to update such old equipment is important for how the security sector, such as the military and police, is modified after a conflict. For example, NATO faced similar challenges in Iraq and Afghanistan, where it led training missions to reform local police and military forces. There, NATO found a unique solution. In countries formerly part of the Warsaw Pact Organization, many units had equipment made in the former Soviet Union. Therefore, troops from the former Central and Eastern Europe were sent to Iraq and elsewhere to maintain and manage local tanks and transport vehicles.

Thus, in the immediate aftermath of the end of the Cold War, there were many grey areas of inter-state relations, spurred on by the rapid post-Cold War expansion of NATO: Ukraine, which was eager to join NATO, sent a force of 1800 personnel to the US-led Multinational Force in Iraq in 2003. Georgia also sent 2000 troops to Iraq in 2007 and actively engaged in joint training with US forces. The inclusion of both countries in NATO's Membership Action Plan (MAP) in 2008 was also part of the US-led Global War on Terror.

4.4.3 Operations Not Assigned by NATO

Alongside the above-mentioned missions that NATO was responsible for, it is also important to note the activities that NATO was not responsible for: according to NATO's official explanation, there are two activities that the alliance was not responsible for: the deployment of NATO troops and the establishment of a No-Fly Zone (No Fly Zone) over Ukraine. Regarding troop deployment, 'the Alliance is responsible for ensuring that this war does not escalate and expand beyond Ukraine'. Regarding the setting of the No-Fly Zone, it is ruled out as involving NATO forces in a direct conflict with Russia.

Why did Ukraine seek to establish a no-fly zone and NATO rule it out? During the civil war in Bosnia and Herzegovina in the former Yugoslavia, which began in

1992, NATO established a no-fly zone and shot down Serb fighters who violated it. This was NATO's first use of force, and since then it has continued to be used to defend the UN "safe areas", eventually extending to the whole of Bosnia. The more full-scale Operation Deliberate Force became a monumental end to the civil war through airstrikes. Four years later, NATO airstrikes also brought fighting to an end in the conflict in the former Yugoslavia over the autonomous province of Kosovo.

What made these NATO airstrikes possible was the superiority of the United States following the collapse of the Soviet Union. It also obtained authorization from the UN Security Council at the time through a resolution authorizing the use of force, which stated that it would "use all necessary means". However, in the current Russo-Ukrainian War, there is no prospect of such a UN Security Council resolution being adopted because Russia is a party to the conflict. There have been cases, such as the Kosovo air strikes, where the use of force was authorized solely by a NATO Council resolution, but there is a risk that international legitimacy may be questioned. In other words, under the current circumstances, it is difficult to justify the establishment of a no-fly zone by a UN resolution authorizing the use of force, and there are significant risks involved in NATO's unilateral declaration. It is therefore considered that the operation was positioned in Ukraine as one that cannot be handled at this time.

4.5 The Alliance's "Capabilities"

The Russian military invasion of Ukraine has significantly changed the role of the Alliance: although it did not result in a direct armed attack on a NATO member state, it threatened the sovereignty and independence of Ukraine as a partner. In this context, NATO established a policy of accelerated forward deployment to prevent the escalation of conflict while supporting Ukraine's national resilience. The question was whether NATO as a whole could assume the capacity to carry out its new mission. It goes without saying that NATO must match its political objectives (missions) with its military means (capabilities).

The decision that the NATO Readiness Force will be responsible for operational operations in the "deterrence and defense" mission for the first time, will it have the capabilities in place to match this? As the strategic theorist Eliot Cohen points out, a more dynamic understanding of the conflict becomes possible if it is not seen as a bilateral conflict between Russia and Ukraine, but between two coalitions of volunteers (Cohen, 2022). Support for the Ukrainian people, who are resisting Russia's military aggression with all their might, is not only extended to the European periphery, but also to NATO and EU member states, and globally. Such support is likely to extend further as the conflict drags on. The support of NATO allies for Ukraine is discussed here, with a focus on their military capabilities.

4.5.1 The NRF's "Deterrence and Defense" Mission

On 24 February, during the Russian military attack on Ukraine, NATO announced that it had activated defense plans to enable the deployment of the NATO Readiness Force, with the NATO Secretary General commenting that "this aggression was not a surprise", as the Alliance had been sharing intelligence and preparing for forward defense readiness. This was due to the fact that it was being done (USDOD, 2022).

Preparations for a 40,000-strong NATO Readiness Force in the north-east and south-east wings of NATO were underway at a rapid pace. The framework was already in place. Following the Crimean crisis, NATO decided to deploy an Enhanced Forward Presence (EFP) against four frontline countries—the Baltic States (Estonia, Latvia and Lithuania) and Poland—as of 2016. The size of the EFP was initially stated to be four battle groups (approximately 5000 personnel), which would be heavily armed with tanks and armored vehicles, and would also be commanded by four allies across the North American continent and the English Channel: the US, UK, Germany and Canada. In other words, the EFP was not directly responsible for forward defense, but was recognized as a "trick line" for launching collective defense.

Alongside these troop deployments in the north-east wing, an agreement on a "Tailored Forward Presence" (TFP) was also reached in the south-east wing as of 2016. However, the content of the TFP was limited to the establishment of a Romanian-led multinational brigade command, adapted to the realities of the Black Sea region, and no concrete troop deployment could be determined, as in the North-East Wing. However, the Russian invasion of Ukraine triggered the decision to deploy a multinational battle group in Romania, Bulgaria, Hungary and Slovakia.

The status of the force deployment is as follows. Included in the north-east wing, in order from north to south, are Estonia (UK-led, 2000 total troops), Latvia (Canadian-led, 1700 troops), Lithuania (German-led, 4000 troops) and Poland (US-led, 10,500 troops) The EFP has increased from its previous size of 5000 troops to more than tripled in size to 18,200.

Next in the south-east wing are Slovakia (Czech-led, 2100 personnel), Hungary (800), Romania (3300) and Bulgaria (900).

These new NATO force formations are supported by troop deployments by member states. Until now, the US has deployed about 7000 troops on a rotational basis, in line with NATO and Russian agreements. However, since February 2022, the US has stepped up to deploy 15,000 more troops, swelling the number of troops in Europe and the US to about 100,000. In addition, more than 1000 troops have been reinforced from the UK to Estonia and Poland, 800 from France and Belgium to Romania and 350 from Germany to Lithuania.

Alongside these forward deployments in the north-east and south-east wings, 130 aircraft and 140 naval vessels are deployed to support NATO's alert posture. In addition, US, British, French, and Italian carrier strike groups have deployed and conducted exercises in the Baltic Sea and the Mediterranean Sea, steadily increasing the visible presence in the land, sea, and air domains. The NATO Alliance is also demonstrating its commitment in terms of capabilities to fulfil its mandate to ensure the sovereignty of member states in their territory, territorial waters and airspace.

4.6 The Alliance's "Division of Labor"

NATO is currently the world's largest alliance with 32 member states, and the division of roles has always been a matter of debate. In order to gain a three-dimensional perspective on how the Russo-Ukrainian War has affected the theory of NATO's division of labor, this chapter discusses it from three perspectives of international politics. Realism, which emphasizes geopolitical conditions; liberalism, which emphasizes Western values and norms; and constructivism, which emphasizes the strategic culture of each country.

First, from the perspective of realism, which emphasizes power and national interests, the geopolitical conditions facing allies are key. In the current crisis, NATO member states bordering Russia (Baltic states and Poland) and NATO member states bordering Ukraine (Poland, Slovakia, Hungary and Romania) reacted most quickly due to security concerns. These countries actively supported the forward deployment of NATO Readiness Force, as discussed in the Alliance's "Capabilities" section. The 180-degree shift in neutrality policy towards early NATO membership by Sweden and Finland, which are becoming increasingly aware of the threat to Russia, may also reflect geopolitical conditions.

Secondly, from a liberal perspective, Russia's invasion of Ukraine is seen as a challenge to the values and norms of liberalism, democracy, rule of law and respect for human rights that NATO and the EU have used as arguments for continuing the enlargement process after the Cold War. The image of Ukrainian citizens continuing to resist for freedom and national self-determination vividly revives the European tradition of patriotism. The outrage against the aggressors who kill "innocent civilians" will never disappear. NATO and the EU will be called upon to maintain an "open door" to such freedom-fighting peoples. From the perspective of liberalism, which emphasizes common values, it can be inferred that the division of roles within the alliance will recede into the background and take on the color of a community of values.

Let us now look at the EU's position, taking a cue from the "Strategic Compass" (European Union, 2022) document published after Russia's invasion of Ukraine. The EU, which now has 27 member states after the withdrawal of the UK, states its "pledge to safeguard the European security order" and puts forward the general principle that "sovereignty, territorial integrity and independence within internationally recognized borders should be fully respected". And it is distinctive in its particular emphasis on international agreements such as the "1975 Helsinki Final Protocol and the 1994 Budapest Memorandum of Understanding" for European countries upset by the Russo-Ukrainian War.

Key to the EU's cooperation with NATO is the military mobility of EU countries, which has so far been supported by the Trans-European Transport Network (TEN-T) initiative, which aims to digitize, improve the cyber resilience of transport infrastructures and their support systems, and enhance artificial intelligence and efficiency in the fields of air and maritime transport are advocated within the framework of the Permanent Military Cooperation Framework (PESCO). The challenges of the Russo-Ukrainian War, such as the mass displacement of people, the efficiency of border crossing procedures and the transport and distribution of humanitarian aid, are widely recognized, and these EU-NATO partnerships will need to be strengthened and the division of roles reviewed.

Finally, from a constructivist perspective, the "strategic culture" of each country is influential. Germany was a strong supporter of pacifism and non-provocative security throughout the Cold War. After the Cold War it gradually expanded its participation in NATO's extraterritorial affairs, shifted to "Responsibility to Defend" and continued to change, including the transfer of Leopard II tanks overseas. The biggest turning point was Russia's invasion of Ukraine. Germany, which until shortly before the invasion had maintained a cautious line compared to the US, Britain and France, drastically changed its previous policy in response to Putin's invasion. Within days of the Russian military invasion, it stepped up the provision of anti-tank munitions and surface-to-air missiles to Ukraine. This was a major shift from the previous policy of not transferring equipment to combat zones.

In order to compare the three "role-sharing" theories of realism, liberalism and constructivism, let us examine them here using statistics from the Ukraine Support Tracker. The initial response by NATO European members was quick. The Ukraine Support Tracker website analyses data on the amount pledged in the approximately three-month period from 24 January to 23 April 2022 in the following three areas. For the first, government support to Ukraine in the financial, humanitarian and military sectors, the top 12 countries are the US, Poland, the UK, Canada, Germany, France, Sweden, Japan, Italy, Luxembourg, Latvia and Estonia, in that order. The amount of aid provided by the top-ranked country, the USA, is approximately EUR 10.3 billion, more than four times the amount provided by the second-ranked country, Poland. However, the total amount of aid provided by the EU institutions and the European Investment Bank is approximately EUR 12.8 billion, which is more than that of the USA. Secondly, looking at this intergovernmental aid as a percentage of GDP, the top 12 countries are Estonia, Latvia, Poland, Luxembourg, Slovakia, Lithuania, Canada, the UK, Sweden, the US, Germany and Slovenia, with the overwhelming majority being EU member states. And finally, a comparison of military aid shows that the top 12 countries are the US, Poland, Canada, the UK, Latvia, Estonia, Slovakia, Italy, Germany, France, Sweden and the Czech Republic. Again, US aid exceeds EUR 3 billion, almost double that of second-placed Poland. Of particular note in Ukrainian aid is the amount of aid provided by Canada in North America. In addition to the large number of Ukrainian immigrants in Canada, it may be noted that there is a strong interest in humanitarian assistance, such as 'Responsibility to Protect' (R2P).

As indicated above, the countries that are actively contributing to Ukrainian assistance this time around largely coincide with those participating in the NATO Forward Defense already outlined. More specifically, the composition overlaps with the countries participating in the Northeast Wing Battle Group deployed in the Baltic States

4 The Impact of the Russo-Ukrainian War on NATO: Implications … 55

and Poland (plus major countries such as the US, UK, France, Germany and Canada) and the Southeast Wing Battle Group.

From the above three perspectives, an overview of the impact of the Russo-Ukrainian War on the division of roles in NATO at the present time suggests that the unprecedented crisis of the Russian invasion of Ukraine, with its shared geopolitical interests, common value norms and national strategic cultures, has significantly changed the nature of the alliance, which may be a common denominator for all three. The three may have something in common. However, it is difficult to assess the ongoing crisis, and more medium- and long-term efforts will be needed in the future.

4.7 Implications for Japan-NATO Cooperation Across the Indo-Pacific Region

Finally, this chapter summarizes the impact of the Russo-Ukrainian Wars on NATO's missions, capabilities and role-sharing, and explore the implications for Japan-NATO partnership.

In terms of the alliance's mandate, the unilateral change of the status quo by Russia has expanded NATO's mandate: NATO has activated its Defense Plan as an alliance, giving NATO Readiness Force for the first time a deterrence and defense mandate. However, in order to control the risk of an escalation of conflict with Russia over the non-member Ukraine, measures such as the deployment of NATO troops to Ukraine and the establishment of a no-fly zone have been foregone. strengthening its resilience at the national level. To this end, NATO member states are providing diverse support to the Kyiv.

In terms of alliance capabilities, they have accelerated forward deployment to what is known as NATO's eastern wing in order to strengthen their deterrence and defense posture against Russia. As the Russian attack went beyond the level of hybrid warfare and became full-scale, with a view to overthrowing the regime, the scope of NATO support was also expanded: the "Article V mandate" for NATO members was repeatedly pointed out, but self-imposed limits were imposed on partner country support.

In terms of the alliance's shared role, common goals, such as improving NATO's readiness to respond and achieving the target of 2% of defense spending as a percentage of GDP, are closer to being realized. The 'strategic culture' of NATO member states is also changing, especially with Germany, which had previously avoided transferring equipment to combat zones, now taking steps to provide anti-tank munitions and surface-to-air missiles. As the Russo-Ukrainian War drags on, NATO may also be required to work with the EU across civil-military boundaries to improve military mobility in the region.

Faced with this "black swan" situation, NATO will continue to adapt the alliance's missions, capabilities and role divisions to the strategic environment. The dramatic change of strategic culture and the alliance management is happening in Japan as well. Almost five months after Russian invasion of Ukraine, Prime Minister Kishida attended NATO Madrid Summit, and expressed his full-fledged support to alliance's new Strategic Concept. It echoed Japan's Free and Open Indo-Pacific (FOIP) concept, in which enhancing connectivity across the region would be mutually beneficial for NATO and Japan. In July 2024, he also attended Washington Summit to celebrate NATO's 75th Anniversary. Japanese leader echoed the importance of the Article 5, which depicts the "extended deterrence", both conventional and nuclear, led by the U.S. So far, NATO's NRF forward deployment and crisis exercises have been successful, and extended deterrence is maintained as an alliance. However, the war situation in Ukraine, where NATO member states border, has not improved and European security remains unstable. And there are doubts as to whether a change of US administration will result in continued support for Ukraine. This is a common challenge for the Indo-Pacific region, and its future will be closely watched. Australia, New Zealand, and Republic of Korea also attended the Washington Summit as Indo-Pacific Four (IP4) members, along with Japan. How the crises in Ukraine will be managed by NATO will be a litmus test for our future alliance.

References

Charap, S., Colton, T. J. (2017). *Everyone loses: The Ukraine crisis and the ruinous contest for post-Soviet Eurasia.* Routledge.

Cohen, E. A. (2022). *Why can't the west admit that Ukraine is winning?* The Atlantic. https://www.theatlantic.com/ideas/archive/2022/03/ukraine-is-winning-war-russia/627121/

Deni, J. R. (2017). *NATO and article 5: The transatlantic alliance and the twenty-first-century challenges of collective defense.* Rowman & Littlefield Publishers.

European Union. (2022). *A strategic compass for security and defence—For a European Union that protects its citizens, values and interests and contributes to international peace and security.*

Freedman, L. (2014). Ukraine and the art of limited war. *Survival, 56*(6).

McDermott, R., et al. (2014, March 5). *Cold war Déjà Vu?* NATO Defense College, Research Report.

NATO. (2016, July 8–9). *"Commitment to enhance resilience," issued by the Heads of State and Government participating in the meeting of the North Atlantic Council in Warsaw.*

USDOD. (2022). *With activation of NATO response force, U.S. military ready to provide forces.*

Open Access This chapter is licensed under the terms of the Creative Commons Attribution-NonCommercial-NoDerivatives 4.0 International License (http://creativecommons.org/licenses/by-nc-nd/4.0/), which permits any noncommercial use, sharing, distribution and reproduction in any medium or format, as long as you give appropriate credit to the original author(s) and the source, provide a link to the Creative Commons license and indicate if you modified the licensed material. You do not have permission under this license to share adapted material derived from this chapter or parts of it.

The images or other third party material in this chapter are included in the chapter's Creative Commons license, unless indicated otherwise in a credit line to the material. If material is not included in the chapter's Creative Commons license and your intended use is not permitted by statutory regulation or exceeds the permitted use, you will need to obtain permission directly from the copyright holder.

Chapter 5
Shifting Trust: Ukrainian Sentiments Towards Social Institutions Before and During War

Olena Akimova and Anna Ishchenko

Contents

5.1	Trust in Social Institutions	59
5.2	Conclusion	66
References		67

Abstract The research highlights the crucial role of trust in social institutions in maintaining social stability, especially during crises. The authors analyze how trust in Ukraine's key institutions, such as the military, state, and local government, has evolved against existential threats from a 2022 Russian invasion. Factors leading to growth in defense-related institutions and fluctuations in trust in political and judicial institutions are central to the analysis. The paper also discusses the transformative impact of wartime on local governance and civil society, where decentralized efforts have proven essential for resilience and rapid response. Trust in regional institutions and volunteer organizations is critical to community cohesion and effective recovery efforts. The authors conclude that maintaining and strengthening trust in social institutions is vital for post-war reconstruction, citizen engagement, and, ultimately, the ability for peace negotiations. However, the sustainable development of trust requires consistent government reforms, transparency, and public participation, supported by national policies and international partnerships.

Keywords Trust · Social institutions · Ukrainians · Ukraine · Citizens · The state

5.1 Trust in Social Institutions

The quality of the relationship between citizens and the state is crucial for the well-being, development, and long-term stability and survival of nations, even during times of peace. However, during times of war, this relationship takes on a unique and

O. Akimova · A. Ishchenko (✉)
Igor Sikorsky Kyiv Polytechnic Institute, Kyiv, Ukraine
e-mail: a.ishchenko@kpi.ua

© The Author(s) 2025
H. Shinoda and P. Ferdorchenko-Kutuyev (eds.),
The Impacts of the Russo-Ukrainian War, SpringerBriefs in International Relations,
https://doi.org/10.1007/978-981-96-2295-5_5

heightened significance. The citizens' respectful attitude toward their state and its core institutions is a key factor in maintaining societal stability, resisting aggression, and ensuring the effective functioning of state institutions, the political system, and the economy.

Trust in social institutions is a key factor in the stability and development of any society. It determines not only the ability of the state to effectively respond to social challenges, but also the degree of consolidation of citizens in difficult periods. In times of peace, trust acts as an indicator of social harmony, but in times of crisis or war, its role becomes crucial for ensuring public support and the stability of public institutions. In the case of Ukraine, the level of trust in basic social institutions has fluctuated significantly during the post-Soviet period, especially during key political events such as the 2004 Orange Revolution and the 2014 Revolution of Dignity.

With the beginning of Russia's full-scale war against Ukraine in February 2022, the trust of Ukrainians in such institutions as the government, army, media, and international organizations began to transform under the influence of new threats and challenges, which is recorded by a number of studies (Tamilina, 2022).

These changes can be explained by a number of factors. Firstly, the key factor is the threat to national security, which unites society and increases the level of trust in institutions that are directly involved in the protection of the state.

In particular, this applies to social institutions that are directly affiliated with the conduct of hostilities and the maintenance of law and order, therefore they are perceived as guarantors of protection against external aggression. For example, according to the data of a sociological study of the Kyiv International Institute of Sociology, the level of trust in the Armed Forces of Ukraine after the start of the war increased to more than 95%, which is one of the highest indicators among all social institutes (Ilko Kucheriv Democratic Initiatives Foundation, 2023). This reaction is typical of societies facing an existential threat, when the army and other defense structures become a symbol of survival and national unity.

In addition, economic difficulties and social instability cause variability in trust in the government and other public authorities. In times of war, the government faces serious challenges in managing the available resources, which in peacetime traditionally directs to maintaining an adequate standard of living—providing the population with basic needs and maintaining economic stability. As a result, trust in government institutions may fluctuate depending on their ability to respond effectively to these challenges. For example, polls show that trust in political power and the government increased in the first months of the war in the wake of unprecedented national unity in the face of existential challenges, but gradually this effect wears off and the economic factor plays a significant role in this.

Another important factor that cannot be overlooked is informational influences and how the informational space of war affects the mass consciousness. It is known that during conflicts, in particular, hybrid wars, the information space becomes a battlefield, where the change in public attitudes can be corrected by the media both in the direction of a positive color and in a polar direction. Coverage of the army's successes, united international support, and unceasing humanitarian and military-technical assistance can be transformed through the media into strengthening support for certain social institutions (for example, the president or the local government).

At the same time, society's vulnerability to misinformation is also evident at this time. This is related to the language factor, when the media content of the enemy can be "consumed" by almost the entire population of Ukraine due to the absence of language barriers, as well as to the effect of deliberate disinformation campaigns.

Last, but not least, is social mobilization and social movements. During the war, the activation of volunteer movements and the role of public organizations has a significant effect on changing public attitudes. In particular, trust is growing in institutions that contribute to the provision of humanitarian aid and support for refugees and victims of war. Public associations that quickly adapt to new conditions and offer effective solutions can increase their support among the population.

With the start of a full-scale Russian war against Ukraine in 2022, Ukrainians' trust in institutions such as the government, army, media, and international organizations began to transform under the influence of new threats and challenges. In particular, data from sociological surveys conducted by the Kyiv International Institute of Sociology (Kyiv International Institute of Sociology, 2022) show that the level of trust in the army has increased significantly, while trust in government and other institutions remained more variable.

The purpose of this study is to analyze changes in Ukrainians' trust in social institutions before and during the war. In particular, we will try to describe what factors really contributed to the growth or decline of the level of trust in certain institutions, as well as what consequences these changes may have for the further development of Ukrainian society in the conditions of the war and post-war reconstruction.

The study of how trust in social institutions is formed and what it affects is the object of many studies. The relationship between social trust and institutional trust is not a self-reinforcing cycle (Daskalopoulou, 2019). It was determined that social trust has a positive effect on institutional trust, in particular in forms of trust in political institutions and supranational political institutions. The same study determined that a negative relationship was recorded regarding the influence of institutional trust on social. It is assumed that there is political trust in a specific group. This argument is further supported by the second key finding of the study, which concerns the presence of a significant effect of time on social and institutional trust. In the context of our survey, the other conclusion that reduced trust in the system activates mistrust of others, because people do not perceive institutions as functioning according to their expectations, becomes particularly important (Daskalopoulou, 2019).

Examining other sources that contain research results on trust formation during crisis situations or during war also allows us to establish some interesting trends. Thus, for example, the experience of civil war generally reduces social trust, especially when people have direct personal experience of violence. This is evident in post-war Kosovo, where the personal experience of war has significantly reduced social trust (Kijewski & Freitag, 2018). And in Nepal, violence during the civil war was found to have reduced trust in national government institutions, underscoring the conflict's detrimental effect on political trust (De Juan & Pierskalla, 2014).

Separate studies are devoted to examining changes in the level of trust in specific vulnerable categories, to which, for example, refugees can be attributed. Thus, some studies show that higher levels of conflict can lead to increased social trust and refugees' trust in certain institutions, such as courts and the police. This may be explained by the positive experience of cooperation during relocation (Hall & Werner, 2022).

In 2015, it was identified that civil wars are transformative forces whose societal consequences depend on the processes that define this collective experience. Thus, according to the results of an international comparative study of the impact of civil war and social trust in 30 post-conflict societies, it was determined that although civil wars reduce trust on average, violence of greater intensity leads to positive changes and greater trust in foreign groups and strangers (Traunmüller et al., 2015). Intense violence during civil wars can sometimes lead to greater trust in outgroups and strangers, suggesting that extreme conflict can foster unexpected social cohesion.

Confidence in the military remains high in post-authoritarian societies, despite a history of violence. This trust is influenced by the support of other political institutions and the role of the military in the fight against crime, as seen in Argentina, Brazil, and Chile (Solar, 2020). During World War II, informal social trust played a significant role in the rescue of Jewish citizens in Nazi-occupied Europe, demonstrating the importance of social trust in collective action during institutional breakdown (Bjørnskov, 2014).

The relationship between war and trust in social institutions is highly context-dependent. Although the existence of conflicts and the level of violence that rises during them usually undermine trust in political institutions, they can sometimes strengthen social trust under certain conditions, for example, through positive experiences of cooperation and increased cohesion. The type of conflict and the role of informal institutions also significantly affect trust outcomes. Understanding these dynamics is critical to post-conflict reconstruction and integration of war-affected populations.

The way Ukrainians perceive their own state, specifically their subjective assessments of its strength and self-sufficiency, has experienced significant fluctuations in recent years. Particularly notable shifts in perceptions occurred during the intense period of large-scale warfare, leading to an unprecedented sense of unity within the nation, including in their assessments of the state. According to surveys conducted by the Institute of Sociology of Ukraine, as of November 2021, there was a noticeable and concerning trend of pessimism in the way people perceived their government in Ukraine. This negative sentiment was prevalent among two-thirds of the population. However, these sentiments shifted dramatically with the outbreak of a large-scale war, when more than 80% of the population began giving positive or neutral assessments of their state. It can be assumed that the war galvanized Ukrainian society to defend its statehood, resulting in a marked improvement in attitudes toward the state. However, this outcome proved unstable, as even substantial societal mobilization failed to yield quick results; instead, the war escalated further. Unfortunately, subsequent developments have indicated a troubling decline in optimism.

By 2023, the number of positive assessments toward the state and its social institutions had dropped by more than half. This decline can largely be attributed to negative systemic events linked to the actions of government officials. War also reshapes the focal points of societal trust in state authorities. Episodes of heroic resistance by the armed forces, coupled with the mere fact that Ukrainian society, the military, and the government endured the initial stages of the war, have further bolstered the already high level of trust in institutions associated with state defense: the Armed Forces of Ukraine, the National Guard, volunteer corps, and the President, who embodies and continues to project the image of an unwavering leader. According to the July 2023 surveys (Razumkov Centre, 2023), among state and public institutions, the most trusted are the State Emergency Service (81%), the State Border Service (78%), the Ministry of Defence of Ukraine (75%), the Security Service of Ukraine (67%), the National Police of Ukraine (61%), the Mayor of the city (township, village) where the respondent lives (60.5%), public organizations (60%), churches (58%), Ukrainian mass media (56%), and the council of the city (township, village) where the respondent lives (55%). However, society also expresses distrust in key institutions responsible for implementing reforms and carrying out effective economic and social protection policies. People in Ukraine tend to distrust courts (the judicial system as a whole, distrusted by 70%), political parties (68%), the state apparatus (officials) (67%), the Prosecutor's Office (60%), the Verkhovna Rada of Ukraine (56%), the National Agency on Corruption Prevention (NACP) (55%), the National Anti-Corruption Bureau of Ukraine (NABU) (54.5%), the Specialized Anti-Corruption Prosecutor's Office (54%), commercial banks (54%), and the Government of Ukraine (52%) (Razumkov Centre, 2023).[1] The results of the surveys indicate that Ukrainian society should simultaneously combat both the external enemy represented by Russian forces and direct efforts towards resolving internal conflicts. This includes implementing measures with the potential for increasing trust in judicial and law enforcement authorities. Distrust in judicial institutions can be considered part of the overall trust in the justice system, which in turn affects confidence in the state's ability to function effectively. Additionally, if people lack faith in fair trials and judicial processes, they may resort to other methods of conflict resolution, such as vigilantism. Given the prevalence of firearms and high incidence of PTSD in the population, such actions can have deadly consequences.

The given data included information on the level of confidence of Ukrainians as of July 2023. However, in order to obtain clearer ideas about the change in the level of trust in the main social institutions in Ukraine, it is necessary to compare these data with the results of the latest research. For the accuracy of the comparison, we will use the data of a similar study conducted by the same institution—the Razumkov Center. First of all, we will identify the main trends that were obtained during the survey in March 2024 (Razumkov Centre, 2024). The key trends according to the sociological research were: a high level of trust in the defense and emergency services,

---

[1] Detailed information at the link: https://razumkov.org.ua/en/sociology/press-releases/citizens-assessment-of-the-situation-in-the-country-trust-in-social-institutions-politicians-officials-and-public-figures-attitude-to-certain-initiatives-of-the-authorities-july-2023.

as well as public and volunteer organizations, a significant level of distrust in political institutions and anti-corruption structures; mixed trust in local self-government. Let's define these trends in more detail with reference to the results.

The Armed Forces of Ukraine have a mostly positive trust rating: 71.2% trust them completely and only 0.9% do not trust them at all, resulting in a significantly high level of trust. The Ministry of Defense is somewhat trusted by 40.8% and completely trusted by 26.7%, which indicates a positive public perception of this government agency related to national security.

Political institutions face significant distrust, which is expressed, for example, in the fact that the Verkhovna Rada of Ukraine has a high level of distrust: 34.4% do not trust at all and only 6.5% trust completely, which leads to a negative balance of trust. The Government of Ukraine and the state apparatus (civil servants): These two also show a noticeable level of mistrust: 29.7% and 35.2% (respectively) do not trust them at all. Both have a negative trust balance, indicating dissatisfaction with national governance and bureaucracy.

Mixed trust in local self-government is expressed in the assessment of the level of trust in the heads of city/village and local councils. These local governments generally perform better than the national ones, with a somewhat positive balance of trust. For example, 40.8% trust local councils to some extent, although the level of complete trust remains low at 10.1% and 7.6%, respectively.

The judiciary and anti-corruption agencies face deep distrust. Negative sentiments show that the public perceives these bodies as opaque and unfair.

Anti-corruption bodies (NABU, Specialized Anti-Corruption Prosecutor's Office, NAZK) have a high level of distrust (from 24.4 to 24.7% do not trust at all) and are perceived negatively, perhaps due to perceptions of inefficiency or corruption within these bodies themselves.

Civic and volunteer organizations are highly trusted. These organizations enjoy some of the highest levels of trust, with 51.5% somewhat trusting and 33.1% completely trusting, resulting in very high overall trust.

Civil society organizations are highly trusted: 51.0% trust to some extent and 10.4% completely trust.

Trust in the Ukrainian mass media is divided: 38.7% partially trust it, but a notable 15.1% do not trust it at all. This creates a relatively neutral balance of trust, reflecting the mixed perception of the media landscape.

The survey shows strong public confidence in defense-related agencies and emergency services, reflecting national solidarity in times of crisis. There is significant public dissatisfaction with national political bodies (such as the Verkhovna Rada and the Government), underscoring the need for reforms to restore trust. Judiciary and anti-corruption institutions need significant improvements to address deep public mistrust and concerns about integrity and efficiency. Local authorities, although more trusted than national authorities, still face some skepticism.

The transformation of trust in local authorities, as well as civil society institutions, is of particular interest in this research. This is primarily due to their key role in ensuring Ukraines' resilience and recovery both during and after the war. The cohesion of society, bolstered by trust in these institutions, demonstrates its ability to rapidly mobilize resources, ensure public oversight, and enhance social adaptation. The period following the full-scale invasion, as well as key episodes during the Orange Revolution and the Revolution of Dignity, showed that one of the main factors in the success of civil society is its close cooperation with local authorities, enabling an effective response to the challenges of war and providing assistance at both the national and regional levels.

In crisis situations, where formal government institutions face resource shortages or temporarily lose their ability to fully function, local initiatives can substitute for these functions and ensure the resilience of the entire system. Local authorities, particularly in regions that have experienced significant destruction, have shown a high level of adaptation to the new conditions. Decentralization, initiated before the war, created opportunities for closer interaction between local governments and citizens, allowing for more rapid responses to needs. However, certain studies point to obstacles in this process, particularly a lack of political will from high-level authorities to engage with civil society in reconstruction (Chatham House, 2024).

Increasing the level of trust in social institutions is a multifaceted process that requires consistent efforts in several areas. It is important to understand that during wartime, many management tools that could be used to build systematic efforts may be unavailable. Therefore, the recommendations outlined here will also include a list of challenges that could slow the achievement of sustainable trust-building outcomes. There are quite obvious factors that can increase the level of trust in social institutions. So, for example, state institutions should enhance their service delivery processes (e.g., healthcare, education, and social support), as this directly impacts the growth of trust in them. Effective service delivery, particularly in critical sectors, improves public perceptions of government competence.

However, there are other, less obvious factors that allow increasing the level of public trust in social institutions. So, for example, involving the public in decision-making contributes to the development of a sense of ownership and trust. Institutions should consult with communities, hold public hearings and invite feedback on major initiatives. Involving the public in decision-making helps develop a sense of ownership and trust.

In the conditions of modern Ukraine, modern digital tools play a significant role in conducting public discussions and involving the public in joint decision-making.

Also an obvious factor is maintaining a robust legal system that applies laws equally to all citizens and upholds justice without bias. Judicial reforms aimed at reducing delays, corruption and inefficiency can help restore public trust.

These listed factors mostly related to the efforts of the state, aimed at strengthening the weak institutions. However, efforts directed at the general public must also be applied. Thus, increasing public awareness of how institutions function and what role they play in society contributes to building trust. Education programs should explain the importance of governance, the rule of law and the system of checks and balances. Thus, educational programs of universities should expand the list of disciplines related to the formation of civic competences, as well as those aimed at the formation of critical thinking skills. With the rise of fake news and misinformation, promoting media literacy is extremely important.

The use of social media for civic activism has a significant positive effect on propensity to trust and trust in institutions such as government, police, and justice systems (Warren et al., 2014). Higher confidence in media abilities and online engagement are associated with increased civic engagement (Park et al., 2023).

Institutes should work closely with non-governmental organizations (NGOs), volunteer groups and community leaders. These organizations often have a higher level of public trust and can act as intermediaries to strengthen institutional trust. Encouraging public participation through volunteer programs in areas such as health, education, and disaster relief can strengthen community-institutional ties. Citizens need to see a long-term commitment to reforms and policies. Frequent changes in leadership or policy can undermine trust. Ensuring consistency of institutional policies and priorities increases stability and reliability. Building trust takes time. Sustained efforts, incremental reforms and positive results will slowly restore trust over time.

Public institutions should have accessible platforms where citizens can voice their concerns or file complaints. These complaints must be dealt with promptly and transparently. Management must respond effectively to public inquiries and demonstrate that it is actively working to resolve issues that affect the community.

In post-conflict situations, providing mechanisms for reconciliation, addressing past injustices and supporting victims can help restore trust. During post-war reconstruction, prioritizing projects that directly affect the daily lives of citizens, such as rebuilding infrastructure, schools, and hospitals, can strengthen trust in public institutions. In times of war, it is especially important that the population trust their leaders and do not question their decisions, especially when those decisions may be unpopular or difficult.

It is important to involve independent bodies or international organizations in the assessment of institutions' activities. Reports from audited external bodies can reassure the public that institutions are functioning properly.

5.2 Conclusion

Summarizing research on changes in public trust in social institutions, it is essential to recognize that trust in government and state institutions forms the foundation for effective post-war reconstruction planning and implementation. When the population trusts government agencies, it facilitates cooperation in rebuilding infrastructure, managing resources, distributing humanitarian aid, and implementing social programs. This is particularly significant in building trust in local authorities, as seen in the de-occupied communities of Ukraine. Since post-war recovery demands joint efforts from various stakeholders, it's equally important to foster trust in other institutions. For instance, voluntary organizations with high credibility can attract more resources and play a more active role in recovery efforts at the community level, enhancing social cohesion and improving the effectiveness of aid—both of which are crucial in the post-war period.

Another critical aspect of trust-building relates to public opinion formation regarding peace negotiations and ending the war. Trust in state institutions, particularly political leadership and bodies representing the population in international forums, influences society's readiness for peace talks. If citizens feel that the government or political institutions overlook their interests or cannot guarantee a just outcome, this can lead to resistance to entering negotiations. In this context, trusted media outlets and civil society organizations play an important role in shaping public opinion on potential peace solutions. They can act as intermediaries between the government and the public, promoting transparency in the negotiation process and alleviating public concerns and mistrust.

In conclusion, a high level of trust in social institutions enhances a country's social resilience, enables more effective resource mobilization for recovery, and supports a constructive negotiation process aimed at achieving sustainable peace. It also fosters greater public consensus on critical decisions during the transition period, contributing to national unity and development.

Acknowledgements In preparing this work, we utilized technical tools, specifically ChatGPT-4o and Grammarly, solely to enhance the clarity and style of written language. These tools were employed to refine language expression without altering the substance or originality of the content.

References

Bjørnskov, C. (2014). Social trust fosters an ability to help those in need: Jewish refugees in the Nazi era. *Political Studies, 63*(4), 951–974. https://doi.org/10.1111/1467-9248.12120

Chatham House. (2024). *Ukraine's wartime recovery: The role of civil society.* https://www.chathamhouse.org/sites/default/files/2024-06/2024-06-05-ukraine-wartime-recovery-role-civil-society-lutsevych.pdf.pdf

Daskalopoulou, I. (2019). Individual-level evidence on the causal relationship between social trust and institutional trust. *Social Indicators Research, 144*(1), 275–298. https://doi.org/10.1007/s11205-018-2035-8

De Juan, A., & Pierskalla, J. H. (2014). Civil war violence and political trust: Microlevel evidence from Nepal. *Conflict Management and Peace Science, 33*(1), 67–88. https://doi.org/10.1177/0738894214544612

Ilko Kucheriv Democratic Initiatives Foundation. (2023). *Results of 2023: Public opinion of Ukrainians.* https://dif.org.ua/article/pidsumki-2023-roku-gromadska-dumka-ukraintsiv

Kijewski, S., & Freitag, M. (2018). Civil war and the formation of social trust in Kosovo: Post-traumatic growth or war-related distress? *The Journal of Conflict Resolution, 62*(4), 717–742. https://www.jstor.org/stable/48597314

Kyiv International Institute of Sociology. (2022). *Public opinion survey results.* https://www.kiis.com.ua/?lang=ukr&cat=reports&id=1441&page=1

Hall, J., & Werner, K. (2022). Trauma and trust: How war exposure shapes social and institutional trust among refugees. *Frontiers in Psychology, 13.* https://doi.org/10.3389/fpsyg.2022.786838

Park, S., et al. (2023). Exploring the relationship between media literacy, online interaction, and civic engagement. *The Information Society*. https://doi.org/10.1080/01972243.2023.2211055

Razumkov Centre. (2023, July 27). *Citizens' assessment of the situation in the country, trust in social institutions, politicians, officials and public figures, attitude to certain initiatives of the authorities*. Press Release. https://razumkov.org.ua/en/sociology/press-releases/citizens-assessment-of-the-situation-in-the-country-trust-in-social-institutions-politicians-officials-and-public-figures-attitude-to-certain-initiatives-of-the-authorities-july-2023

Razumkov Centre. (2024, March). *Assessing the situation in the country, trust in social institutions, belief in victory, and attitude to elections*. Press Release. https://razumkov.org.ua/en/sociology/press-releases/assessing-the-situation-in-the-country-trust-in-social-institutions-belief-in-victory-and-attitude-to-elections-march-2024

Solar, C. (2020). Trust in the military in post-authoritarian Societies. *Current Sociology*. https://doi.org/10.1177/0011392120969769

Tamilina, L. (2022). Key features and factors behind social trust formation in Ukraine. *East European Politics and Societies: And Cultures*, 088832542211153. https://doi.org/10.1177/08883254221115303

Traunmüller, R., Born, D., & Freitag, M. (2015). How civil war experience affects dimensions of social trust in a cross-national comparison. *SSRN Electronic Journal*. https://doi.org/10.2139/ssrn.2545816

Warren, A. M., Sulaiman, A., & Jaafar, N. I. (2014). Social media effects on fostering online civic engagement and building citizen trust and trust in institutions. *Government Information Quarterly, 31*(2), 291–301. https://doi.org/10.1016/j.giq.2013.11.007

Open Access This chapter is licensed under the terms of the Creative Commons Attribution-NonCommercial-NoDerivatives 4.0 International License (http://creativecommons.org/licenses/by-nc-nd/4.0/), which permits any noncommercial use, sharing, distribution and reproduction in any medium or format, as long as you give appropriate credit to the original author(s) and the source, provide a link to the Creative Commons license and indicate if you modified the licensed material. You do not have permission under this license to share adapted material derived from this chapter or parts of it.

The images or other third party material in this chapter are included in the chapter's Creative Commons license, unless indicated otherwise in a credit line to the material. If material is not included in the chapter's Creative Commons license and your intended use is not permitted by statutory regulation or exceeds the permitted use, you will need to obtain permission directly from the copyright holder.

Part II
Agendas for Durable Peace in Ukraine

Chapter 6
The Scope of the Ripeness Theory in the Russo-Ukrainian War

Hinako Yasui and Hideaki Shinoda

Contents

6.1	Introduction	72
6.2	Events Leading to the Donbas War	72
6.3	Who Were the Parties to the Conflict?	74
6.4	Ripeness Theory	75
	6.4.1 Ripeness	75
	6.4.2 Mutually Hurting Stalemate (MHS)	76
	6.4.3 Ripeness and Third-Party Intervention	76
	6.4.4 Limitations of Ripeness Theory	76
6.5	Was the War Ripe Before the Minsk Protocol?	77
6.6	Prospects	78
References		79

Abstract The Ripeness theory of I. W. Zartman gives a clue to imagine conditions for the termination of the Russo–Ukrainian War. While the theory only provides a vision of the end of the war in an abstract manner, it still helps us to illustrate key issues to bring an end to the War. To achieve ripeness as the basis of negotiations for peace agreement or ceasefire, it is imperative to identify the state of MHS (mutually hurting stalemate). In the case of the Russo–Ukrainian War, there was a moment of ripeness during the Donbas War. But Russia's increasing involvement which eventually led to its full-scale invasion collapsed ripeness.

Keywords I. W. Zartman · Ripeness · MHS (mutually hurting stalemate) · Russo–Ukrainian war · Donbas war · MEO (Mutually Enticing Opportunity) · Way-out · Minsk agreements

---

H. Yasui
Tokyo University, Tokyo, Japan
e-mail: suningkid@gmail.com

H. Shinoda (✉)
Tokyo University of Foreign Studies, Tokyo, Japan
e-mail: hshinoda@tufs.ac.jp

© The Author(s) 2025
H. Shinoda and P. Ferdorchenko-Kutuyev (eds.),
The Impacts of the Russo-Ukrainian War, SpringerBriefs in International Relations,
https://doi.org/10.1007/978-981-96-2295-5_6

6.1 Introduction

Since Russia's full-scale invasion of Ukraine began on February 24, 2022, hostilities between the two countries have continued, with no clear signs of an end to the war, at the time of writing this chapter in October 2024. Unless one side achieves complete victory through the annihilation of the other, a peace agreement, or at least a ceasefire, will be necessary. Even if Ukraine regains all the territories that Russia has invaded and occupied, some form of agreement with Russia will still be required if both parties are to cease fighting.

Therefore, it is essential to consider the possible ways in which the war might end. One well-known theory regarding mediation for the resolution of conflicts is I. W. Zartman's "Ripeness Theory". This theory introduces two key concepts: the "ripeness of the conflict" and the "Mutually Hurting Stalemate" (MHS), which suggest that serious discussions aimed at ending the conflict can take place when the timing is appropriate. (Zartman, 2003, 2019).

This chapter is intended to examine the war between Russia and Ukraine through the lens of the Ripeness Theory. However, it does not exclusively focus on the War after 24 February 2022. Instead, this chapter explores the history of conflicts between the two countries, particularly after the "annexation" of Crimea and the outbreak of the Donbas War in 2014. By doing so, the chapter argues that it may be useful to view the Russo–Ukrainian War in the context of the Donbas War, beginning in 2014. It is widely accepted that the failure of the two Minsk agreements contributed to the full-scale invasion in 2022, though Russia and Ukraine have markedly different interpretations of that failure. This chapter offers a perspective on a decade of conflict, starting in 2014, using Zartman's Ripeness Theory as a framework.

First, the chapter briefly reviews the history of the Donbas War in relation to the ongoing Russo–Ukrainian War. It then applies Zartman's Ripeness Theory to the Donbas War, highlighting key factors that contributed to the failure of the two Minsk agreements. Finally, the chapter discusses possible insights from the Ripeness Theory in the context of the current Russo–Ukrainian War.

6.2 Events Leading to the Donbas War

The causes of war are always complex and controversial, and the Donbas War is no exception. This chapter does not seek to analyze the specific causal factors of the war but aims to place it within the broader context of the long-standing conflict between Russia and Ukraine, in order to better apply theoretical perspectives like the Ripeness Theory.

After winning the 2010 Ukrainian presidential election, then-President Viktor Yanukovych pursued closer relations with Russia, a direct contrast to the policies of his predecessor, Viktor Yushchenko, who had prioritized ties with Europe (Hattori, 2018). Alongside an economic downturn and growing dissatisfaction with corruption surrounding Yanukovych, there was significant opposition to his anti-EU stance (Hattori, 2018). In November 2013, a pro-Western, anti-government movement emerged to usher in a political turmoil, known as the "Maidan Revolution". This movement led to Yanukovych's ouster and the resignation of his cabinet in February 2014. In the wake of the revolution, a provisional government was formed, with Arseniy Yatsenyuk, leader of the "Fatherland" party, as prime minister. The interim government included members of the nationalist, anti-Russian "Freedom" party, which drew a strong response from Russia, which contested the legitimacy of the new government. In the presidential election of May 2014, Petro Poroshenko, who had served as foreign minister under Yushchenko, was elected president, further reinforcing Ukraine's nationalist and pro-Western orientation (Hattori, 2018).

In response to the Maidan Revolution, separatist activity intensified in eastern Ukraine, where many pro-Russian forces were based (Matsuzato, 2023). In Donetsk and Luhansk, "people's governors" were elected, following Crimea's example, becoming leaders of the separatist movement. In Donetsk, Pavel Gavrilov, a Russian nationalist and advertising company owner, was elected; in Luhansk, Alexander Kharitonov, the regional secretary of the Progressive Socialist Party of Ukraine (PSPU), was elected; and in Kharkiv, Vladimir Varshavsky, a car mechanic and blogger, was chosen. In early March, separatists occupied government buildings, but local police quickly regained control. However, tensions escalated as the conflict between separatists and the Ukrainian government grew.

On 6 April, 2014, separatists in Donetsk again seized the administrative building, declaring the establishment of the "Donetsk People's Republic" (DPR) the next day. Separatists in Luhansk followed suit, proclaiming the "Luhansk People's Republic" (LPR) on April 27. Separatist forces, led by Igor Girkin, also captured administrative buildings in Slavyansk, Kramatorsk, and Krasnyi Liman. In response, the Ukrainian government launched the "Anti-Terrorist Operation" (ATO), deploying troops to regain control of separatist-held areas.

The First Battle of Donetsk Airport, which began with a Ukrainian airstrike on 26 May 2014, marked a turning point, ending in a Ukrainian victory. From June to early July, the Ukrainian government force regained key positions in Mariupol, Bakhmut, and Slavyansk, pushing the separatists to a critical point. In response to the Ukrainian offensive, Russia gradually increased its involvement. In July, Russia provided military supplies and support, and even shot down Ukrainian transport planes and fighter jets. By August, Russia's regular army had entered the conflict, dealing heavy blows to the government of Ukraine.

In September, a ceasefire was brokered by the Organization for Security and Cooperation in Europe (OSCE) between Ukraine and Russia with the DPR and the LPR. However, the ceasefire was soon violated with the outbreak of the Second Battle of Donetsk Airport later that month. The battle dragged on until January of the following year, when the Ukrainian force was finally forced to withdraw. Around the same time, the Ukrainian force lost the Battle of Debaltseve, compelling the government of Ukraine to sign the Minsk II agreement, which included conditions more favorable to Russia, particularly granting broader autonomy to Donetsk and Luhansk.

6.3 Who Were the Parties to the Conflict?

Identifying the conflict parties in the Donbas War is challenging due to the complexities of the relationships among various stakeholders. It is also controversial, as Ukraine and Russia have differing views about the nature of the war.

At the beginning of the Donbas War, it could be argued that one party was the Ukrainian government, while the other consisted of eastern separatist groups such as the DPR and LPR, with Russia acting as a supporter of the separatists. However, from around July 2014 (though the exact timing may be debated), Russia began conducting military operations with its own troops and providing training to the separatists. This marked Russia's transition into a clear and significant party to the conflict. The separatists would not have been able to sustain the fighting without Russia's support. The alignment of Ukraine opposing Russia and the separatists mirrors the situation in the war that began in 2022.

Despite the two Minsk Agreements and varying levels of military confrontations, it is widely believed that the Donbas War had never truly ended prior to Russia's full-scale invasion in 2022. Thus, it may be argued that the Donbas War never ended and has, in fact, continued alongside the Russo–Ukrainian War after the beginning of the full-scale invasion. Another possible way to understand the situation is by conceptualizing the two wars as the same one. Alternatively, the Donbas War may have been absorbed into the larger, overt conflict between the two countries. In either case, the two wars are interconnected, having merged, as events on the ground evolved. It is symbolic that the signatories of Minsk I included Ukraine, Russia, the DPR, and the LPR, while the signatories of Minsk II were only Ukraine and Russia. Well before 2022, when many considered the war to be an internal conflict within Ukraine rather than a war between two nations, the distinction between the intra-state war and the future international war was already increasingly blurred over time.

A conflict can be defined as "a state that occurs when multiple parties pursue incompatible goals" (Shinoda, 2021 and Ramsbotham et al., 2016). Thus, the identification of conflict parties depends on the distinctiveness of each stakeholder's goals. What were the incompatible goals of Russia and Ukraine? First, it is clear that Ukraine's goal in the Donbas War was to "maintain Ukraine's independence and territorial integrity", For Ukraine, a young nation that emerged from the collapse of the Soviet Union, territorial integrity is the foundation of its sovereignty. In contrast, the goals of the DPR, LPR, and Russia were less clear. Initially, the DPR and LPR appeared to be separatist groups seeking independence from Ukraine and other nations. However, it soon became evident that they were heavily dependent on Russia, and there were indications that they aspired to be integrated into Russia. Russia's objectives were also ambiguous, often shifting. On one hand, Russia appeared to be protecting pro-Russian populations in Ukraine. On the other, it seemed to have ambitions to exert more direct influence over eastern Ukraine through the DPR and LPR.

Identifying the conflict parties in the Donbas War is not the main focus of this chapter. However, it is important to emphasize that, due to the ambiguity surrounding the distinctness of the two wars and the parties involved, the two conflicts are intrinsically interconnected, making it difficult to clearly demarcate them. Therefore, instead of viewing the two wars as coexisting, it would be more appropriate to understand them as intertwined, with their boundaries difficult to distinguish.

6.4 Ripeness Theory

Next, we will outline the ripeness theory, which serves as the framework for our analysis in this chapter. The theory suggests that the ripeness of a conflict is crucial for the initiation of peace negotiations, a concept advanced by American political scientist I. William Zartman in the 1980s. While many studies on peace negotiations and mediation focus on the contents of agreements, his ripeness theory stands out in emphasizing the timing of peace negotiations as key to their success (Zartman, 2000: 225–226). Since the time the theory was initially proposed, the ripeness theory has been the subject of extensive research by numerous scholars (Pruitt, 2005; Stedman, 1991). In this chapter, we will focus on the work of Zartman (2000).

6.4.1 Ripeness

Zartman explains the theory of ripeness through six propositions. The first proposition is: "Ripeness is a necessary but not sufficient condition for the initiation of negotiations, whether bilateral or mediated." (Zartman, 2000: 227) According to Zartman, when a conflict has ripened and reached a "ripe moment", serious negotiations toward a peace agreement become possible. However, he warns that some negotiations might be driven merely by external pressure, and the initiation of talks alone does not guarantee that the conflict is ripe for resolution (Zartman, 2000: 227).

So, what defines the moment of ripeness in a conflict? In his second proposition, Zartman states that "If the parties to a conflict (a) perceive themselves to be in a hurting stalemate and (b) perceive the possibility of a negotiated solution (a way out), the conflict is ripe for resolution". (Zartman, 2000: 228–229) The first element, the perception of a "hurting stalemate", refers to the idea of a mutually hurting stalemate (MHS), a central concept in ripeness theory, which occurs when all parties recognize they have reached an impasse. The second element, "the possibility of a negotiated solution", indicates that the parties see a potential for resolution through negotiation. Zartman calls this a "sense of a way out". (Zartman, 2000: 228).

6.4.2 Mutually Hurting Stalemate (MHS)

Zartman elaborates on the conditions for the first elementMHS—in the third proposition. He explains that "An MHS contains objective and subjective elements, of which only the latter are necessary and sufficient to its existence" (Zartman, 2000: 229). The objective element is the actual stalemate in the conflict, but an MHS is formed only when the parties subjectively recognize and accept its development. Zartman asserts that the subjective recognition of the stalemate is the critical factor, meaning that no matter how much objective evidence exists concerning a deadlock or the high costs of conflict, an MHS will not arise unless both sides acknowledge it. Conversely, even if the objective signs of a stalemate are weak, if the parties subjectively feel the "hurt", an MHS can still emerge (Zartman, 2000: 229).

Zartman also notes that MHS is based on a "cost–benefit analysis". In a "cost–benefit analysis", used in policy planning, the "benefits" and "costs" of a project are weighed to determine its viability. In a conflict, for an MHS to be recognized, both parties must rationally compare the costs and benefits of continuing the fight.

Summarizing this, Zartman states in his fourth proposition that "If the parties' subjective expressions of pain, impasse, and inability to bear the costs of further escalation, related to objective evidence of stalemate (e.g., casualties and material costs), are present, along with a sense of a way out, ripeness exists (Zartman, 2000: 231).

6.4.3 Ripeness and Third-Party Intervention

In the fifth proposition, Zartman discusses the role of a mediator in advancing peace negotiations once ripeness is established. He suggests that "(a) Once ripeness has been established, specific tactics by mediators can seize the ripe moment and turn it into negotiations; (b) If only objective elements of ripeness exist, mediators can bring the conflicting parties to recognize their mutual stalemate and initiate negotiations". (Zartman, 2000: 232) In cases where conditions for ripeness are in place, mediators must act swiftly to seize the opportunity for talks. In the second case, when only objective elements of ripeness exist, mediators may need to persuade the parties to recognize the stalemate and bring them to the negotiating table.

6.4.4 Limitations of Ripeness Theory

Zartman's first proposition emphasizes that ripeness is a condition for initiating negotiations, not for their success or failure. The theory addresses factors that lead to the start of peace talks but does not guarantee their continuation or success. In ripeness theory, an MHS and a sense of a way out are preconditions for initiating negotiations. However, once negotiations begin and hostilities cease, the objective elements that form the basis of the MHS may dissolve, causing the MHS itself to disappear[1] (Sticher, 2022).

To address this limitation, Zartman introduces the concept of a Mutually Enticing Opportunity (MEO) in his sixth proposition. He states: "The perception of a mutually enticing opportunity is a necessary but not sufficient condition for the continuation of negotiations to the successful conclusion of a conflict" (Zartman, 2000: 243). According to Zartman, an MEO gives the conflicting parties hope during negotiations. If the transition from MHS to MEO is managed effectively, negotiations are more likely to succeed. Although Zartman does not specify the conditions for the establishment of an MEO, he implies that for parties seeking benefits, the "enticing opportunity" is the prospect of gaining something from peace negotiations. Creating such opportunities requires political adjustments to balance the interests of the parties involved.

6.5 Was the War Ripe Before the Minsk Protocol?

What observations can we derive by applying Zartman's Ripeness Theory to the Donbas War and the Russo–Ukrainian War? First, none of the Minsk agreements were able to produce lasting peace, and the ceasefire was repeatedly broken. According to the ripeness theory, this was because the agreements were concluded when the conflict was not yet ripe. In other words, there appeared to be two moments during the Donbas War when ripeness seemed to have arrived, but both failed as the assessments of those moments were mistaken. The misjudgment of ripeness was not due to a miscalculation of the military balance on the ground in Ukraine but rather due to the arrival of Russian forces. In short, the moment of ripeness may have occurred during the course of the Donbas War, but Russia's intervention disrupted it.

A conflict becomes ripe when "the parties (a) recognize they are in a stalemate and have been hurt, and (b) recognize the possibility of a negotiated solution (a way out)". The conflict between Ukraine and Russia did not meet these requirements for a mutually hurting stalemate (MHS) or a sense of a way out. First, regarding the MHS, while Ukraine had suffered significantly by 2015, Russia had not been hurt enough to feel cornered. Only the DPR, which was supported by Russia, experienced a stalemate during the Second Battle of Donetsk Airport, but the regular Russian army was never in a similarly desperate position, and there was no nationwide mobilization as seen after the 2022 invasion. Therefore, in 2015, only Ukraine was suffering, making it difficult to argue that both sides were equally "hurt".

Regarding the second requirement, the sense of a way out, Ukraine did not meet this condition. Ukraine's primary objective was to recover its territory, and any situation in which Russia maintained influence, as recognized in the Minsk agreements,

---

[1] In this regard, Sticher states that ceasefires do not necessarily prevent the maturation of conflicts, and that depending on the length and timing of the ceasefire, they may even promote maturation.

was unacceptable. Furthermore, the significant military power disparity between Russia and Ukraine meant that the two could not negotiate on equal terms. From Ukraine's perspective, the Minsk agreements did not reflect its original goals, making it hard to envision how the situation could be resolved through those negotiations. In contrast, Russia was able to safeguard its interests through negotiations (i.e., it perceived a way-out), while Ukraine could not achieve its own objectives through the same process (i.e., it did not perceive a way-out). Therefore, the Donbas War, which lacked both MHS and a sense of a way out, was not ripe for resolution, making the failure of the Minsk agreements almost inevitable.

From this perspective, Russia's full-scale invasion of Ukraine in 2022 can be seen as a possible consequence of the unresolved Donbas War, if not an inevitable result. The potential moment of ripeness during the Donbas War was undermined by Russia's intervention, which viewed the conflict as part of a broader regional struggle involving Russian interests, rather than a purely internal Ukrainian conflict. Once Russia intervened, it became clear that ripeness could not be achieved. Identifying the moment of ripeness requires careful observation of the situation on the ground and a clear understanding of the conflict parties' goals. When the configuration of conflict parties shifts and an internal conflict becomes an international one, the identification of ripeness obviously breaks down.

6.6 Prospects

This chapter has argued that the transformation of the Donbas War to the full-scale invasion was a transition process. The chapter illustrated the implications of the observation by applying the ripeness theory to the conflicts over Ukraine after 2014. If there were two separate wars, it would have been the case that the moments of ripeness would come separately twice. But the reality betrayed this expectation at the time of the collapses of the two Minsk Agreements that were supposed to settle the Donbas War. The original seemingly internal war gradually changed its nature to transform itself into an outright international war. Whatever the views about the initial nature of the Donbas War and the assessment of Russia's involvements at the initial stage are, it is apparent that the initial war developed gradually and intensively from 2014 to 2022. That is the fundamental structural factor that obstructed the achievement of the moment of ripeness and led to the collapse of the Minsk Agreements.

The implication of this observation is clear. Ukraine needs to intensify its capability to confront the intervention by Russia and then should be able to bring about a moment of ripeness. According to Jesper Sjöberg, the Russo–Ukrainian War from 2022 onwards is a situation that could be considered MHS, given the objective material losses (Sjöberg, 2023). Despite the initial advancement of the Russian forces in February 2022, the Ukrainian forces continued to regain lost territories after March 2022. The so-called counter-offensive around the summer of 2023 brought about additional gains for Ukraine. But then the apparent stalemate became evident. This situation is one step closer to the ripeness of the conflict than the situation in the

Donbas War, in that it has made Russia feel MHS. This is largely due to the support of Western countries. Unfortunately, since the time of the Ukraine's advancement in the Kursk province in August 2024, the stalemate began to melt down. It seemed that Ukraine resisted the consolidation of the stalemate regardless of the risks entailed in its Kurs operation.

Without the economic and military support of Western countries, the MHS would not have occurred due to the absolute power gap between Russia and Ukraine. In order to bring the war between Russia and Ukraine closer to ripeness and stability to the region, it will be essential for Western to establish a system to provide support to Ukraine during and after the war. But in the end, if the conflict parties resist the consolidation of ripeness regardless of risks, they could continue to avoid it.

References

Hattori, M. (2018). *Ukuraina Wo Shirutame No Rokujuugo Shou [65 Chapters to Learn about Ukraine]*. Akashi Shoten (in Japanese).
Matsuzato, K. (2023). *Ukuraina Douran—Soren Kaitai Kara Rousennsou Made [Ukrainian Upheaval—From the Soviet Demise to Russio-Ukrainian War]*. Chikuma Shobou (in Japanese).
Pruitt, D. G. (2005). *Whither ripeness theory?*. George Mason University Working Paper 25.
Ramsbotham, O., Woodhouse, T., & Miall, H. (Eds.) (2016). *Contemporary conflict resolution*. Polity.
Shinoda, Hideaki. (2021). *Funoskaikets towa nandarou (What is conflict resolution)* Chikumashobo (in Japanese).
Sjöberg, J. (2023). NFaktorer För Framgångsrik Medling i Postsovjetiska Konflikter: - En utvärdering, analys, och jämförelse av Georgienkriget och Ukrainakriget utifrån ripeness theory [Factors for successful mediation in post-Soviet conflicts—An evaluation, analysis, and comparison of the Georgian and Ukrainian wars based on ripeness theory]. Umeå University. https://www.diva-portal.org/smash/record.jsf?pid=diva2%3A1774840&dswid=-4751. Accessed on October 22, 2024.
Stedman, S. J. (1991). *Peacemaking in civil war: International mediation in Zimbabwe, 1974–1980*. L. Rienner Publishers.
Sticher, V. (2022). Healing stalemates: The role of ceasefires in ripening conflict. *Ethnopolitics* https://doi.org/10.1080/17449057.2022.2004776. Accessed on October 29, 2024.
Zartman, W. (2000). Ripeness: The hurting stalemate and beyond. *International conflict resolution after the cold war*. National Academy Press. https://nap.nationalacademies.org/read/9897/chapter/7. Accessed on October 20, 2024.
Zartman, W. (2003). Understanding ripeness: Making and using hurting stalemate. In R. M. Ginty, & A. Wanis-St. John (Eds.), *Contemporary peacemaking: Peace processes, peacebuilding and conflict*. Palgrave Macmillan.
Zartman, W. (2019) *I William Zartman: A pioneer in conflict management and area studies: Essays on contention and governance*. Springer.

Open Access This chapter is licensed under the terms of the Creative Commons Attribution-NonCommercial-NoDerivatives 4.0 International License (http://creativecommons.org/licenses/by-nc-nd/4.0/), which permits any noncommercial use, sharing, distribution and reproduction in any medium or format, as long as you give appropriate credit to the original author(s) and the source, provide a link to the Creative Commons license and indicate if you modified the licensed material. You do not have permission under this license to share adapted material derived from this chapter or parts of it.

The images or other third party material in this chapter are included in the chapter's Creative Commons license, unless indicated otherwise in a credit line to the material. If material is not included in the chapter's Creative Commons license and your intended use is not permitted by statutory regulation or exceeds the permitted use, you will need to obtain permission directly from the copyright holder.

Chapter 7
Security Guarantees as Balancing Ukraine with Russia: Reflections on Geopolitical Theories

Hideaki Shinoda

Contents

7.1	Security Guarantees as Balancing	82
7.2	Two Traditions of Geopolitical Theories	83
7.3	Continental Tradition of Geopolitical Theory	84
7.4	Anglo-American Tradition of Geopolitical Theory	87
7.5	John Mearsheimer's Offensive Realism	88
7.6	Henry Kissinger and Modifications of Balance	90
7.7	Balance for a Ceasefire Agreement	92
7.8	Balance in the Post-Russo–Ukrainian War Era	96
7.9	Concluding Remark	98
References		98

Abstract The discussions about "security guarantees" for Ukraine need to take into consideration a large picture of the balance of power to introduce mechanisms to deter further Russian aggressions. Theories of geopolitics and international relations represented by Halford Mackinder, Karl Haushofer, John Mearsheimer, and Henry Kissinger are of importance to visualize such a large picture of balancing. Balance for a ceasefire would not contradict legitimacy for a peace agreement. Flexible manners of introducing multilayered "security guarantees" are required in the large picture of the balance of power.

Keywords Security guarantees · Balance · Balance of power · Legitimacy · Mackinder · Haushofer · Mearsheimer · Kissinger · Geopolitics · Geopolitical theory

---

H. Shinoda (✉)
Tokyo University of Foreign Studies, Tokyo, Japan
e-mail: hshinoda@tufs.ac.jp

7.1 Security Guarantees as Balancing

The government of Ukraine together with NATO, EU, and G7 partner countries, has been discussing "security guarantees" as a blueprint for achieving stability after the war with Russia. These security guarantees are intended to align with the "Peace Formula" and the "Victory Plan" (Herasymchuk & Badrak, 2023; Milles, 2023; Tallis, 2023). A series of bilateral agreements with partner countries has been introduced so far, outlining the nature of each partner's assistance. While it is undoubtedly important to secure various forms of assistance from these partners, it remains unclear how these individual bilateral agreements will be integrated into a cohesive and overarching framework of security guarantees. Discussions in policy circles often result in multiple lists detailing the various forms of assistance that partner countries can provide to Ukraine. However, this approach tends to divert attention from the overarching goal of these efforts.

This chapter seeks to identify the overall goal of these "security guarantees" as establishing and maintaining a balance between Ukraine and Russia in terms of military power and other relevant capabilities. Without such a balance, it will be difficult to prevent future invasions, regardless of how territorial boundaries are drawn. Conversely, if this balance can be maintained, a stable status quo, characterized by mutual deterrence, may be achievable. Thus, maintaining a balance of power is the fundamental basis for long-term stability under the framework of "security guarantees."

To pursue this vision of "security guarantees" as a means of establishing a balance, this chapter begins by examining the classical geopolitical theories of Karl Haushofer and Halford Mackinder. Haushofer, representing the "Continental" school of geopolitical thought, is particularly relevant to the worldview of contemporary Russia under Vladimir Putin. Mackinder, on the other hand, represents the "Anglo-American" tradition of geopolitical theory, which underpins the worldview of NATO members. These geopolitical theories offer insights into potential modes of "balance" and will serve as a foundation for examining the concept of "security guarantees."

Next, the chapter turns to two major theorists in the field of International Relations: John Mearsheimer and Henry Kissinger, both of whom have made specific remarks on the Russo–Ukrainian conflict from theoretical perspectives. Mearsheimer has provided extensive commentary on the geopolitical situation involving Russia and Ukraine, particularly since 2014, when he began criticizing NATO's eastward expansion. In contrast, while Kissinger has not focused specifically on the conflict between Russia and Ukraine, he has made occasional illustrative remarks on the broader geopolitical landscape.

Finally, this chapter will explore the current structural confrontation between the "West" and the "non-West" in the contemporary international community, integrating these theoretical perspectives to deepen our understanding of the discussions surrounding "security guarantees".

7.2 Two Traditions of Geopolitical Theories

This chapter has argued that there are two major traditions in the history of geopolitical theory (Shinoda, 2023). One is based upon the Continental tradition of political philosophy in which states are perceived to be organic entities. They have their own living spaces too. The other is derived from the Anglo-American tradition of political theory in which states are the products of social contracts. They tend to pursue contractual relationships among like-minded states too. Both have rich histories in political philosophies and international theories (Shinoda, 2000). This chapter suggests that the worldview typically associated with Russian political theory derives from the Continental geopolitical tradition, while NATO's attraction to Ukraine stems from the Anglo-American geopolitical tradition. Although this chapter does not delve into the details of these two traditions, it is useful to highlight some of their key features before discussing the two major theorists of geopolitics, Karl Haushofer and Halford Mackinder.

Haushofer's theory, developed in Germany, contrasts sharply with Mackinder's theory, developed in Britain. In Mackinder's theory, the "geographical pivot of history" is centered on the land power of the Heartland, which inevitably pursues expansionist policies (Mackinder, 1942). The sea powers surrounding this "pivot" adopt containment strategies in response, and history unfolds as a result of this dynamic. Mackinder's worldview is binary, presenting the world as divided between land powers and sea powers, with forces of expansionism clashing with forces of containment. These can also be understood as revisionist powers versus status quo powers, or as territorial expansionists versus those prioritizing networks.

In contrast, Haushofer's theory envisions a world characterized by multiple zones, divided into several spheres of influence, each dominated by a powerful entity. In this worldview, the critical issue is which state has the strength to secure its own "living space" (*Lebensraum*), how far that space should extend, and how relationships between different living spaces are maintained. Stability arises when hegemonic powers respect each other's territories. When one hegemonic power encroaches on another's living space, it disrupts the order.

Mackinder's theory aligns with the ideological tradition and political interests of the Anglo-American world. For sea powers, containing expansionist forces that threaten the status quo is essential to national interests. Thus, maintaining a universalist stance and upholding the network they belong to, even in peacetime, becomes crucial. Sea powers that promote principles such as freedom of the seas and free trade also have an interest in preserving an international order based on territorial integrity and the prohibition of the use of force. This is the logical outcome of Mackinder's theory.

On the other hand, Haushofer's theory aligns with the ideological tradition and political interests of continental powers like Germany. In each regional order, the hegemonic nation-state seeks to establish its own living space. To maintain stability, it is necessary for these powers to respect the living spaces of other nations while asserting dominance within their own region. The world, in Haushofer's view, is composed of multiple regional spheres of influence, which exist through the mutual recognition of living spaces. This is the logical conclusion of Haushofer's *Pan-Ideen* theory.

Thus, Anglo-American geopolitics and Continental geopolitics differ fundamentally in their worldviews. Each theory is based on a perspective of the world that leads to vastly different policy prescriptions. Mackinder's geopolitics highlights the structural conflict between two geopolitical communities—land powers and sea powers—shaped by geographical conditions. It also points to the types of policies that align with the universalist worldview held by sea powers. In contrast, Haushofer's geopolitics emphasizes the organic connection between nations and their specific territories, recognizing the existence of distinct living spaces for powerful political communities. It suggests policies that align with a pluralistic worldview, where multiple living spaces coexist and interact.

The divergence between these two geopolitical theories runs deep, grounded in conflicting worldviews, each claiming to be objectively based on geographical realities (Shinoda, 2023).

	Anglo-American geopolitics	Continental geopolitics
Representative figures	Halford Mackinder	Karl Haushofer
Keywords	Heartland, Sea Power, Land Power, Rimland, Bridgehead	*Lebensraum* (Living Space), *Pan-Ideen* (Pan-ideas), *Geopolitik*
Characteristics	Emphasis on geographical conditions, freedom of the seas, focus on containment of land power by sea power	Organic theory of the state, emphasis on great powers, aims for an order based on the existence of multiple zones
Worldview	Binary worldview	Pluralistic worldview
Ideological tendency	Compatible with twentieth century international law, universalist, globalist, liberal	Nostalgic for nineteenth-century European public law, anti-universalist, anti-liberal
Policy tendency	Alliance network extension	Zone-oriented expansion/coexistence

7.3 Continental Tradition of Geopolitical Theory

It was Karl Haushofer, a professor of geography at Munich University, who coined the term *Geopolitik* (geopolitics) and attempted to establish it as an academic discipline. Haushofer was the intellectual successor to German geopolitical thought, building on the work of Friedrich Ratzel and Johan Rudolf Kjellén (Shinoda, 2023). He began his career as a military officer, serving as an artillery regiment commander on the Western Front during World War I. During the interwar period, he transitioned to academia, lectured on policy, and became closely aligned with the Nazi regime, eventually becoming part of Germany's policy-making community. However, following

World War II, suspicion of his involvement in Nazi war crimes led him to commit suicide. Despite his systematic work in legitimizing *Geopolitik* as a geopolitical theory, Haushofer's deep association with German nationalism and his personal history have relegated him to the shadows of geopolitical history.

Haushofer's connection with the Nazis does not have to be too much overemphasized. As he had a Jewish wife, Haushofer did not espouse anti-Semitic views. He was a strong advocate of the German-Japanese alliance, though he did not favor conflicts with the Soviet Union or the United Kingdom. His connection to Hitler came through Rudolf Hess, a founding member of the Nazi Party, who took dictation for Hitler's *Mein Kampf*. The concept of *Lebensraum* (living space), a central part of Hitler's expansionist ideology, was what Haushofer influenced Hitler, as Haushofer provided this idea to Hitler with Hess. Later, Hitler used the notion of *Lebensraum* to justify military expansion. The understanding of a nation as an organic entity tied to a specific geographic territory was central to Haushofer's *Geopolitik*, which he inherited from Ratzel and Kjellén. If Haushofer was not involved with anti-Semitic views, he was involved with *Lebensraum*.

Germany, being the largest ethnic group in Europe, historically lacked a unified political community with its own land. This longing for a union between nation and territory resonated deeply with the German spirit, and Haushofer's *Geopolitik*, which theoretically explained this sentiment, held strong appeal for Hitler. Haushofer's notion of *Lebensraum* involved expansive zones tied to spheres of influence, or "pan-regions", as articulated in his 1931 essay *Geopolitik der Pan-Ideen* (Haushofer, 1931), In Continental geopolitics, the concept of *Raum* (space) was essential. If a specific "space" was linked to a nation-state, then a broader geographic area, or *Pan*, represented a larger regional sphere. Haushofer's *Pan-Ideen* (pan-ideas) envisioned these vast regions as ideal zones of influence. This "sphere theory," which emphasized the interaction of multiple spheres of influence, was a hallmark of Continental geopolitics.

In Haushofer's view, the Soviet Union's interior constituted a *Lebensraum*, as did Japan's claim over East Asia and the Western Pacific. His theories appealed to many Japanese, particularly during the 1930s and 1940s, when the idea of the Greater East Asia Co-Prosperity Sphere gained prominence in Japan. The United States, according to Haushofer, was the hegemon of the Western Hemisphere, while Germany, if it established its own *Lebensraum*, would dominate Europe. Following Kjellén's ideas, which resembled social Darwinism, Haushofer assumed that powerful nations naturally dominated vast regions. In his view, each major power should respect the *Lebensraum* of other powers to maintain international stability. The idea of a single nation ruling the entire world contradicted the natural order and was not rooted in his geopolitical theory. Thus, leading powers within each pan-region should recognize each other's spheres of influence to avoid disaster.

After the Cold War with the collapse of the USSR, Russia's power was diminished. But later in the twenty-first century, Russia regained power and its expansionist policies resurfaced, particularly through figures like Aleksandr Dugin, a proponent of "Eurasianism" (Dugin, 2015; Shekhovtsov, 2008). Following Russia's full-scale invasion of Ukraine in 2022, the ideology of "Eurasianism" continued to be widely discussed. Dugin advocated for the annexation of Ukraine, arguing that a cultural and political community centered on Russia exists in the heart of Eurasia. This community, according to Dugin, naturally includes not only Central Asia and the Caucasus but also former Soviet bloc countries like Ukraine. This belief resonates with the tone of President Putin's 2021 essay, "On the Historical Unity of Russians and Ukrainians", which suggested that Russians and Ukrainians share a common ethnic heritage, implying that Ukraine should be part of Russia (President of Russia, 2021). The essay played a significant role in justifying the military invasion that followed in 2022.

Putin and Dugin, in a sense, embrace the concept of the sphere of influence or *Lebensraum*, challenging the post-Cold War international order that disregards spheres of influence. They argue that international stability can only be achieved when hegemonic powers within each sphere of influence recognize one another. From their perspective, if Russia's sphere of influence diminished after the Cold War and the collapse of the Soviet Union, it is Russia's right to restore it. If the international community, especially Western countries, refuses to acknowledge this restoration, it is seen as an injustice. Many Russians, including Putin, subscribe to this worldview, which has shaped Russia's actions in Ukraine.

Putin frequently claims that the West is responsible for the war. He accuses other nations of wrongdoing simply for rejecting Russia's worldview, which conflicts with the established international order. The international order, as established by the United Nations Charter, is based on principles of sovereign equality and the self-determination of peoples, leaving no room for the concept of *Lebensraum* or spheres of influence. Even the idea that Ukrainians and Russians share an ethnic origin does not justify Russia's annexation of Ukraine. The normative system of the Charter of the United Nations, born from the collapse of Nazi Germany's *Lebensraum* and Imperial Japan's Greater East Asia Co-Prosperity Sphere, rejects such ideologies. It may be the case that this system is largely based on the network-oriented Anglo-American geopolitical theory. Still, the UN Charter provides the fundamental principles of contemporary international society. The Continental geopolitical theory, exemplified by Russia's actions, acts as a destabilizing force in such a normative system.

In this sense, the Russia–Ukraine War can be seen as a conflict between the Anglo-American geopolitical tradition, which supports the established international order, and the Continental geopolitical tradition, which seeks to challenge it. For Ukraine to deter Russia's aggression, it is imperative to set up the mechanism to contain the expansionism based upon the Continental tradition of geopolitical theory in line with the Anglo-American tradition of geopolitical theory. The balance ought to be sought even between the frameworks of the two traditions of geopolitical theories.

7.4 Anglo-American Tradition of Geopolitical Theory

Halford Mackinder's 1904 paper, "The Geographical Pivot of History", is considered a foundational work in the field of geopolitics (Mackinder, 1942), even though Mackinder himself refrained from labeling his work as such. His essay was likely influenced by contemporary global events, particularly the Russo–Japanese War, which broke out just months after Mackinder delivered the lecture at the Royal Geographical Society in Britain that would later evolve into the essay. Mackinder, a British geographer, was deeply interested in international politics, especially the rivalry between Russia—a key adversary in Britain's "Great Game"—and Japan, Britain's ally in the Anglo-Japanese Alliance, in the Far East. Despite his own reluctance to be called a scholar of "geopolitics", Mackinder is today recognized as one of the most significant figures in the Anglo-American tradition of geopolitical theory.

The central insight of Mackinder's paper was the identification of a special area in the heart of the Eurasian continent, which he termed the "heartland". This vast area, protected by the uninhabited Arctic to the north, is insulated from invasions, giving it a unique geopolitical advantage. At the same time, however, the heartland's geographical isolation—being largely landlocked and lacking accessible rivers to the open sea—posed limitations. Ports, if constructed, would often be frozen in winter, cutting off maritime access for much of the year. This isolation became a key factor in Mackinder's theory, and it contributed to his reputation as a preeminent geopolitical thinker.

According to Mackinder, the states within the heartland would naturally seek to overcome these geographical limitations by expanding southward. A powerful land power in the heartland, particularly with military strength, would inevitably aim to project its influence across the Eurasian continent, shaping the course of global politics. Mackinder viewed Russia's southward expansion as the "pivot of history", driven by these fundamental geographical constraints.

Another major contribution from Mackinder was his distinction between land power and sea power. He argued that states in the continental interior, like those in the heartland, were oriented toward land power, while those surrounded by seas, like Britain, embodied sea power. Unlike land powers, which are driven to expand across continents, sea powers have ready access to the oceans and can benefit from trade without needing to conquer vast territories. However, if a land power were to obstruct a sea power's access to the oceans, it would present a significant threat, prompting the sea power to adopt containment strategies. This land-sea power dichotomy became a defining feature of Mackinder's geopolitics, particularly as it played out in the nineteenth century during the "Great Game" between Britain and Russia. Mackinder viewed the Anglo-Japanese Alliance, formed to counter Russian expansion in the Far East, as a prime example of this dynamic.

Mackinder's global vision further divided the world into geographical regions. The Heartland formed the central continental area, surrounded by an "inner crescent" of territories adjacent to it. Beyond this lay the "outer crescent" of islands, which included major sea powers like Britain, Japan, the United States, Canada, and

Australia. Strategic "bridgeheads," such as the Indian subcontinent and the Korean Peninsula, became crucial areas where land powers and sea powers would clash for influence.

Mackinder's ideas were later developed by American geopolitical thinker Nicholas Spykman, who expanded on Mackinder's framework. Spykman shared Mackinder's view that international politics was essentially a contest between land and sea powers. However, Spykman emphasized that sea powers focused more on containing land powers rather than establishing their own defined spheres of influence. He introduced the concept of the "rimland", a term to describe the peripheral regions of Eurasia that serve as access points from the sea, where both land powers and sea powers vie for control. Spykman also introduced the idea of "amphibia," states in the rimland that possess characteristics of both land power and sea power. His theories significantly influenced U.S. foreign policy during the Cold War.

The formation of NATO reflects the influence of the Anglo-American geopolitical theories of Mackinder and Spykman. NATO was an alliance of sea powers and coastal allies, designed to contain the Heartland power of the USSR. NATO's creation underscored the binary worldview that was typical of Anglo-American geopolitics, dividing the world between land powers and sea powers. In the 1990s, following the end of the Cold War, NATO's eastward expansion became a matter of intense debate. Although NATO eventually incorporated former communist Eastern European and Southern European states, it stopped short of admitting countries from the former USSR area. This restraint was rooted in a tacit acknowledgment of the Continental tradition of geopolitics, which emphasized spheres of influence.

However, the question of Ukraine's potential accession to NATO is now illuminating this geopolitical tension. Ukraine's bid for NATO membership has become a flashpoint in the conflict between the Anglo-American tradition of global containment and the Continental tradition, which emphasizes spheres of influence and respect for zones of power. This conflict reflects a broader clash of worldviews, deeply embedded in geopolitical theory, that continues to shape contemporary international relations. A kind of balance should be identified to avoid the clash as a result of such a direct confrontation of the two worldviews of the two traditions of geopolitical theories. In order to explore it, the chapter turns to two major theorists of international relations, John Mearsheimer and Henry Kissinger.

7.5 John Mearsheimer's Offensive Realism

John Mearsheimer, a leading figure in the field of International Relations and a proponent of "offensive realism", has sparked substantial debate regarding NATO's eastward expansion and the West's approach to Ukraine. Mearsheimer argues that Western nations, by pushing NATO, the EU, and democratic ideals into Ukraine, have effectively undermined Ukraine's role as a "buffer state" between Russia and the West. He predicted as early as 2015 that Russia would take aggressive action if Ukraine continued to align more closely with the West. This view became especially relevant after Russia's full-scale invasion of Ukraine in 2022, further validating Mearsheimer's belief that NATO's increased military cooperation with Kyiv triggered Moscow's escalatory response.

Mearsheimer contends that the closer Ukraine moved toward NATO, the more Russia perceived it as a direct threat. He criticizes Western diplomacy, suggesting that rather than deterring Russia, it provoked President Putin's actions. However, Mearsheimer does not embrace conspiracy theories that suggest the 2014 Maidan Revolution was orchestrated by Western intelligence. He does, however, argue that Ukraine's strategic importance to the United States is overstated. From his perspective, Ukraine should have been preserved as a buffer state between Russia and NATO, as this would have reduced the likelihood of conflict. In his realist view, the United States should have refrained from trying to bring Ukraine into NATO, since Russia considers Ukraine part of its sphere of influence.

Mearsheimer's analysis also examines the shifting political dynamics within Ukraine. Before 2014, the country's political forces were divided between pro-Russian factions, predominantly in the east, and pro-European factions in the west. But after the Maidan Revolution, Russia's "annexation" of Crimea, and the ongoing conflict in eastern Ukraine, the balance shifted. With Russia securing its influence in the east, Ukraine's central government moved towards a more pro-European and pro-NATO stance. Mearsheimer believes that this shift marked the end of Ukraine as a buffer state and that Western military support for Ukraine has only deepened the geopolitical rift (Mearsheimer, 2014a).

Despite his adherence to offensive realism, Mearsheimer's argument does not align with the principles of contemporary international law, which does not mandate that Ukraine or any other sovereign nation must remain a buffer state. His critique reflects a worldview that prioritizes great power politics reminiscent of Europe in the eighteenth and nineteenth centuries. This form of geopolitics is based on spheres of influence and balance-of-power dynamics, which Mearsheimer suggests are still relevant in today's world. In his framework, international legitimacy is derived from the influence and dominance of great powers rather than adherence to international law.

Mearsheimer frequently invokes the "Monroe Doctrine" to explain the nature of American foreign policy. He argues that all great powers seek to dominate their own region and prevent other powers from doing the same in theirs. According to this logic, the United States seeks to maintain hegemony in the Western Hemisphere, just as it did through the Monroe Doctrine in the nineteenth century. For Mearsheimer, NATO's expansion after World War II can be seen as an extension of the Monroe Doctrine into Europe, aimed at preventing powers like Russia or Germany from dominating the continent. However, he criticizes excessive U.S. involvement in regions outside the Western Hemisphere, suggesting that such interference risks provoking overreactions from regional powers like Russia (Mearsheimer, 2022).

In his influential book *The Tragedy of Great Power Politics*, Mearsheimer also predicted the rise of China as a global superpower, asserting that the future structure of international politics would be shaped by U.S.–China rivalry (Mearsheimer, 2014b).

He draws a parallel between U.S. dominance in the Western Hemisphere and China's potential efforts to dominate Asia. Just as the U.S. has worked to exclude rival powers from the Americas, China would naturally seek to push the U.S. out of Asia. In this context, Mearsheimer believes that it would have been more strategically sound for the U.S. to enlist Russia as a counterbalance to China, rather than escalating tensions over Ukraine. From his viewpoint, the U.S.-Russia conflict over Ukraine is an unnecessary distraction from the more critical geopolitical competition with China.

Mearsheimer's geopolitical framework bears a striking resemblance to the theories of Karl Haushofer. Both Mearsheimer and Haushofer share the belief in the importance of regional dominance. Where they differ is in Mearsheimer's more fluid conception of power, where great powers not only dominate their own regions but also seek to obstruct rivals from achieving regional hegemony elsewhere. Haushofer's influence also resonates with the contemporary BRICS alliance, which promotes a multipolar world order with Brazil in Latin America, Russia in Central Eurasia, India in South Asia, China in East Asia, and South Africa in Africa—a concept that echoes Haushofer's division of the world into distinct spheres of influence.

In essence, Mearsheimer's "offensive realism" presents a challenge to contemporary international relations theory, particularly the principles that emphasize international law and multilateralism (Ikenberry, 2001). His insistence on the persistence of great power politics underscores a broader struggle in the modern world between different geopolitical visions: one, exemplified by the U.S.-led NATO alliance, that seeks a rules-based international order, and another, rooted in the realist tradition, that prioritizes regional hegemony. His controversial remarks about Ukraine as a buffer state are all based upon the observation of the seriousness of the confrontation between the two camps.

But is it then inevitable that Ukraine as a country must be a buffer state entirely? Is there any room for more nuanced manners of alleviating the confrontation? In order to examine these questions, the chapter now turns to Kissinger.

7.6 Henry Kissinger and Modifications of Balance

Henry Kissinger's remarks at the World Economic Forum at Davos in May 2022 caused a stir, as he was said to advocate for Ukraine to make territorial concessions to Russia. This prompted critical responses from Ukrainian Foreign Minister Dmytro Kuleba and President Volodymyr Zelenskyy. There had been opinions suggesting that Ukraine should accept surrender, and Kissinger's remarks were hastily categorized as supporting such a stance. Often labeled a "realist", Kissinger might have been seen as advocating a standpoint similar to that of John Mearsheimer. While it is true that he had previously referred to Ukraine as a "neutral state" and argued that Europe's balance could not be achieved by excluding Russia, his actual view was more nuanced.

At Davos, Kissinger began by referring to the situation in Ukraine as an event symbolizing a historical transformation, predicting that its outcome would influence future international relations. He recalled that, eight years prior, he had suggested that Ukraine might ideally become a "neutral kind of state" serving as a "bridge between Russia and Europe." In other words, he envisioned Ukraine not as a frontline state of Europe. However, Kissinger suggested that while this might remain the goal, it is no longer viable in the same way. According to him, peace negotiations needed to begin within a few months, but the relationship between Russia, Georgia, Ukraine, and Europe would not be easily resolved. Ideally, "Ideally, the dividing line should return the status quo ante" (World Economic Forum, 2022).

This reference to "the dividing line returning to the status quo ante" was interpreted by many as suggesting Ukraine should surrender its territories. However, Kissinger also stated that "modifications to that dividing line may occur during the negotiations, which, of course, have not yet been established." Such modifications, he said, would be challenging, as they should reflect Ukraine's efforts during the war and "wisdom for the balance in Europe and in the world at large". In other words, Kissinger stated that the status quo ante should be pursued, but it must account for the new realities on the ground in accordance with the war's developments.

In an interview with the German magazine *Spiegel* in July in the same year, Kissinger denied the misunderstanding. He emphasized that he never advocated territorial concessions and that Ukraine should not make any in the first place. He explained that he had merely pointed out that "the logical dividing line for a ceasefire is the status quo ante" (Spiegel International, 2022).

Kissinger's terms are distinctive. He did not necessarily say which side was good or evil, or which should win the war. Instead, he discussed "modifications" of "balance" in relation to newly observed "legitimacy," seeking to identify conditions for a ceasefire within a broader European context. Kissinger emphasized that the relationship between Europe and Russia must be set in a way that goes beyond Russia's current regime. For 400 years, Russia has constituted part of "Europe's balance" in various forms. It is important, he noted, not to drive Russia into a permanent alliance with China. He also remarked that, in recent years, the United States and China have developed a special relationship. Given the new "balance" emerging from the Russo–Ukrainian War, countries such as Iran with its nuclear ambitions, fragmented Middle Eastern nations, and others like India and Brazil must be integrated into the international system.

In making these points, Kissinger did not offer a conclusive direction, which may have led to the misunderstanding. However, he emphasized that the dividing line should be pursued through negotiations that reflect the new realities on the ground. He outlined a guiding principle for restoring the status quo ante. First, he believed that Ukraine should ideally be a "neutral state" between Europe and Russia. Second, due to the ongoing war, it has become increasingly impossible to treat Ukraine as a "neutral state" in the same way as before, and thus a certain "modification" is necessary. Third, since this "modification" would be difficult—and would depend on the outcome of the war—Kissinger did not propose specific details. However, he asserted that the "modification" must be carried out by major actors, including Ukraine, in a way that restores the "balance of Europe". This necessity, he argued, arises from the broader global context, meaning that Europe's balance must be situated within the framework of global dynamics.

It is clear that Kissinger did not simply advocate surrendering territories, though his reference to "modification" remains somewhat ambiguous. He attached conditions to this "modification." The first condition is that Ukraine's heroic actions must be acknowledged. Ukraine has shown brave resistance and is fighting effectively against the full-scale invasion of a military power like Russia. Moreover, its conventional military capabilities continue to improve. Given these facts, it would be unrealistic to demand that Ukraine revert to its previous "neutral state". The second condition is that "Europe's balance" must be restored with Russia as a participant. Pursuing peace by excluding Russia could undermine Europe's balance. Russia will not simply disappear from Europe due to the war. The third condition is that "Europe's balance" must be assessed within the global context. It is impossible to consider Europe's balance without including the United States. Likewise, it would be unrealistic to ignore China's influence. While the degree of influence varies, the actions of other non-European countries must also be considered in restoring Europe's balance.

7.7 Balance for a Ceasefire Agreement

Those who misunderstand Kissinger's statements hold a strong preconception that ending the war and resolving political issues must be achieved simultaneously. However, considering the differences between a "ceasefire agreement" and a "peace agreement," it becomes clear that the cessation of hostilities and the end of a state of war are distinct. For example, the Korean War is still technically ongoing, with only a ceasefire in place. According to William Zartman's "ripeness theory" discussed in the previous chapter, a "Mutually Hurting Stalemate (MHS)" makes a ceasefire more likely. However, to end a war with a political resolution, another significant step must be taken. If we do not recognize the continuity between a ceasefire agreement and a peace agreement, we cannot create a broader peace process. Expecting to achieve a ceasefire and a peace agreement completely and simultaneously could lead to an unnecessary continuation of hostilities. We should maintain a medium- to long-term perspective, considering the moment of "ripeness" while also grasping the current situation.

If resolving a conflict aims to secure long-term stability, it is desirable that the resolution aligns with principles shared not only by the parties involved but also by surrounding countries and other stakeholders. If it does not align with the international legal order, it may temporarily cover up the issue, but it tends to lead to instability over time. Since 2014, the situation in Ukraine has shown that principles of modern international society, as outlined in the UN Charter—such as the prohibition of the use of force, sovereign equality, self-determination, and non-interference in domestic affairs—have been violated. To aim for a long-term political resolution, the principle of "legitimacy" in international society must be emphasized. Even if complete restoration of "legitimacy" is not achieved upon entering a ceasefire, abandoning "legitimacy" itself could hinder long-term stability.

It is crucial to identify "ripeness" or "balance" to capture the moment for a ceasefire. If legitimacy follows, it is also possible to seek a peace agreement. Both balance and legitimacy are important, and it is desirable to have both together side by side. However, balance may need to be established first for a temporary ceasefire, if possible. Then, a long-term settlement with solid legitimacy could be sought.

In Ukraine's case, the "annexations" of Crimea and the eastern territories contradict international "legitimacy." Forcing the Ukrainian government to recognize such situations would be tantamount to compelling it to violate international principles. This approach should not be taken. However, if the parties agree to enter a ceasefire with the understanding that a long-term political resolution will be entrusted to future negotiations, this is a state that may need to be accepted. Maintaining "legitimacy"—the core principles of international society—will be a crucial link between a ceasefire agreement and a peace agreement, i.e., the cessation of hostilities and the resolution of political issues. However, this must be implemented in relation to reality within a specific time frame.

In 1932, after occupying northern China militarily, the Imperial Japanese Army established "Manchukuo". The United States, viewing this as an illegal "puppet state" established in violation of the 1919 Covenant of the League of Nations and the 1928 Kellogg-Briand Pact, declared that it would never recognize "Manchukuo". This declaration, known as the "Stimson Doctrine" after then-U.S. Secretary of State Henry Stimson, is well-known. Japanese people at that time tended to perceive this as a hostile U.S. policy toward Japan rather than as a doctrine. While it is true that this attitude by the U.S. was not something imagined by the international law of nineteenth-century Europe, the principle of not recognizing realities born out of illegal circumstances adopted by the U.S. became a standard general principle in post-World War II international society. The "Stimson Doctrine" symbolizes the framework of the international order from the twentieth century onward. The attitude of rejecting "Manchukuo", denying colonial rule, and insisting on maintaining "legitimacy" in international society underpins the post-World War II international order. In the case of Ukraine, even if a ceasefire agreement is reached without ending Russia's occupation of Crimea and the eastern regions, the "legitimacy" of international society would not be restored, necessitating continued political negotiations to ensure "legitimacy."

Of course, merely advocating for "legitimacy" will not end the war. Only with real power backing the principle of "legitimacy" would effectively contribute to political stability. In the aforementioned interview, Kissinger states: "the balance of power is a precondition for other things, but it is not an end in itself. The balance of power by itself does not guarantee stability, but without balance of power, you cannot have stability" (Spiegel International, 2022).

Before being appointed National Security Advisor by President Richard Nixon, Kissinger was a professor at Harvard University. The foundation of his academic career was his research on the Congress of Vienna in 1815 after the Napoleonic Wars, which he explored while writing his doctoral dissertation, *A World Restored*. In this research, Kissinger meticulously depicted how European countries, reeling from the chaos of the Napoleonic Wars, restored order through diplomatic negotiations during the Congress of Vienna. He focused on Austrian Foreign Minister Klemens von Metternich and British Foreign Minister Viscount Castlereagh, analyzing their diplomatic efforts to restore "legitimacy" and "balance" (Kissinger, 2013). Metternich was dedicated to restoring Europe's "legitimacy", as represented by the construction of the Holy Alliance. In contrast, Castlereagh was committed to restoring the "balance of power" among the great powers through the adjustment of complex international relations. Kissinger concluded that it was these diplomatic efforts by individuals of outstanding ability that brought about the restoration of order in Europe through "legitimacy" and "balance".

Kissinger's remarks on the Ukrainian situation at Davos also follow this pattern. From his perspective, the collapse of the Soviet Union and NATO's eastward expansion disturbed the "balance" in Europe. Kissinger seems to think that the "legitimacy" of Ukraine is connected to its "neutrality" between Russia and Europe, which has been disrupted. As a result, he suggested "modification" is required to restore the "balance of Europe". In doing so, Kissinger also implied that, given Ukraine's resilience shown during the war, it would no longer be treated simply as a neutral state. At the same time, the "balance" of Europe ought to be restored with Russia's involvement. Moreover, this "balance" must be established within a global context. These were the implications of Kissinger's remarks at Davos.

In his masterpiece, *Diplomacy*, in the immediate aftermath of the Cold War, Kissinger expressed concern about the future of post-Soviet Russia. He emphasized that throughout much of Russian history, Russia has always sought opportunities for expansion. In 1994 Kissinger warned against the American tendency to place excessive hope in Russia's democratic reforms, influenced by Wilsonian idealism.

> Students of geopolitics and history are uneasy about the single-mindedness of this approach. They fear that, in overestimating America's ability to shape Russia's internal evolution, America may involve itself needlessly in internal Russian controversies, generate a nationalist backlash, and neglect the usual tasks of foreign policy. They would support a policy designed to modify Russia's traditional truculence and would for that reason favor economic aid and cooperative projects on global issues. They would argue, however, that Russia, regardless of who governs it, sits astride the territory Halford Mackinder called the geographical heartland, and is the heir to one of the most potent imperial traditions. Even were the postulated moral transformation to occur, it would take time, and in that interlude America should hedge its bets. (Kissinger, 1994: 814)

He added that even if a moral transformation were to occur in Russia, it would take time, and in the meantime, U.S. should spread its risks. While alleviating Russia's suffering and encouraging economic reform is an important tool of U.S. foreign policy, "they are not, however, substitutes for a serious effort to maintain the global balance of power vis-à-vis a country with a long history of expansionism" (Kissinger, 1994: 814).

In other words, Kissinger was highly skeptical of an approach that sought to establish a peaceful international order through changes in domestic politics brought about by democratization. He argued that, in addition to "legitimacy," the maintenance of order through "balance" should also be considered. This was due to his insight that Russian expansionism is a deep-seated tradition observed from the perspective of Mackinder's geopolitical theory.

In 1994, Kissinger observed that the dominant geopolitical thrust has been Russia's attempt to restore its pre-eminence in all the territories formerly controlled from Moscow. In the nature of peacekeeping, Russia seeks to re-establish some form of Russian tutelage. The overwhelming majority of Russia's leaders "refuse to accept the collapse of the Soviet Empire or the legitimacy of the successor states, especially of Ukraine, the cradle of Russian Orthodoxy." (Kissinger, 1994: 815).

Kissinger further commented that Russia has special security interests in what it calls the "near abroad" or the republics of the former Soviet Union. For the sake of world peace, these Russian interests must be addressed without military pressure or unilateral military intervention. He argued that policymakers should prepare for potential future trends and not rely solely on domestic reforms. "Russian reform will be impeded, not helped, by turning a blind eye to the reappearance of historic Russian imperial pretentions. The independence of the new republics, recognized after the United Nations, must not be tacitly downgraded by acquiescence in Russian military moves on their soil." (Kissinger, 1994: 818).

Kissinger was acutely aware of the security concerns felt by Eastern Europeans. He understood that the "vacuum" in Eastern Europe needed to be filled. The Visegrad countries—Poland, the Czech Republic, Hungary, and Slovakia—would become no man's land between Germany and Russia, if they do not belong to the EU and NATO. At the time, the U.S. government was still reluctant to expand NATO eastward, but Kissinger advocated for it. President Bill Clinton argued against their membership, asserting that NATO cannot draw a new line of division in Europe that presupposes future confrontations between East and West. Kissinger criticized Clinton's stance, remarking that the U.S. must avoid creating a strategic and theoretical vacuum in Eastern and Central Europe under the guise of preventing confrontation. Later, the Clinton administration shifted its position, achieving NATO's eastward expansion in its second term from 1997, a move strongly supported by Kissinger.

From a foreign policy standpoint, Kissinger's core argument was that the U.S. could not rely solely on internal reforms within Russia and that a balance was necessary given Russia's traditional expansionism. Leaving Eastern European countries in a "security vacuum" would likely provoke Russian expansionism. Thus, NATO expansion was the only way to ensure balance, a belief Kissinger held firmly in 1994. Notably, however, his vision of NATO expansion at the time did not include Ukraine.

In 2022 Kissinger still viewed international order as sustained by legitimacy and balance, while he also suggested the necessity of "modifications". If the system is fixed permanently, Ukraine may have to remain a buffer state, as propagated by Mearsheimer. But Kissinger indicates "modifications", as he implies that there are more flexible manners of making a balance without keeping Ukraine a buffer state permanently. In the end what is important is not making Ukraine a buffer state, but maintaining the balance of power in Europe and the world by including Ukraine as a key actor. Kissinger believed that ignoring the balance of power would make new confrontations inevitable. But it seems that the way the balance of power is maintained should constantly changes. His realist approach, rooted in the belief that both "legitimacy and balance" remains the same, although the new reality of the Russo–Ukrainian War would have to change the calculation of the balance.

7.8 Balance in the Post-Russo–Ukrainian War Era

Having observed the theoretical perspectives relevant to our task, this chapter summarizes that balancing is key in "security guarantees". John Mearsheimer argues that unless Ukraine becomes a buffer state, halting Russian advances will be impossible. This perspective is rooted in geopolitical theories emphasizing spheres of influence. Conversely, Henry Kissinger contends that adjustments can be made to balance mechanisms, given Ukraine's strengthened position and support from its partners. The containment of sea power alliances could further expand based on a different calculation of power configurations. Both theoretical frameworks offer insights into the balance of power in the region. A shared understanding is clear: a balance to sustain the cessation of hostilities must be derived from a broader analysis of the regional and global balancing mechanisms.

It is true that balancing two opposing forces is a challenging task that requires not only battlefield engagements but also efforts across various sectors of society. Russia is larger than Ukraine in terms of military size, territory, population, Gross Domestic Product (GDP), and natural resources. Therefore, establishing a balance between Russia and Ukraine is inherently difficult. Thus, however, internationally broader pictures are necessary.

To compensate for the disparities with Russia, Ukraine relies on support from the United States and its allies. With the backing of multiple partners within the "Western" camp, Ukraine may sustain a stalemate and achieve a balance with Russia. Bilateral agreements between Ukraine and its partner countries serve as additional resources to maintain this balance. Regardless of whether Ukraine is able to regain all its original territories by force, the necessity of establishing a balance with Russia remains unchanged. A significant challenge is the lengthy border between Ukraine and Russia; controlling this extensive boundary—spanning thousands of kilometers—in a conventional manner is extremely difficult, if not impossible. Addressing painful issues such as the establishment of buffer zones between the two countries and the installation of landmines along the border cannot be avoided. The management of multi-layered zones would have to be considered to better maintain the balance between Ukraine and Russia.

Given the anticipated long-term hostility between the two countries, it is logical for Ukraine to seek membership in NATO and the EU to effectively balance against Russia. However, the path to joining NATO or the EU is fraught with challenges, including technical obstacles and political objections. It is particularly difficult for Ukraine to gain acceptance from these regional organizations during the ongoing conflict and shortly thereafter. The lack of regional mechanisms for Ukraine inevitably leads to a reliance on bilateral arrangements. For now, Ukraine must focus on developing "security guarantees" with key partners without immediate accession to NATO or the EU. Even if Ukraine eventually joins these organizations, there will need to be special provisions regarding the application of Article 5 (collective self-defense) of the North Atlantic Treaty in buffer zones and other specific areas. Additionally, there are concerns regarding potential countermeasures from the anti-NATO/EU bloc. For instance, the BRICS initiative for "de-dollarization" aims to mitigate the impact of economic sanctions imposed by the U.S., EU, and their allies on adversaries like Russia. Thus, accession to NATO and the EU should not be viewed as a panacea, as both organizations have limited capacities.

Japan is one of the countries that have strongly supported Ukraine, even though it is not a member of NATO or the EU. Former Prime Minister Fumio Kishida often remarked on the linkage between Indo-Pacific security and Euro-Atlantic security. He suggests that, given the critical security situation in East Asia, Japan should contribute to European security affairs to ensure that like-minded countries within the U.S. alliance network pay attention to security in East Asia. Although Japan does not provide lethal weapons to Ukraine due to domestic legal constraints, it has contributed significantly through humanitarian and development aid. The notion that the scope of the "Free and Open Indo-Pacific (FOIP)" initiative should extend to the Euro-Atlantic region has been warmly received by Japanese policymakers, although concrete examinations of this idea are still forthcoming. Since Ukraine faces the Black Sea, which connects to the Indian Ocean and Pacific through critical maritime routes such as the Mediterranean Sea, Red Sea, and Arabian Sea, the linkage between Indo-Pacific security and Euro-Atlantic security warrants more concrete exploration to ensure that the balancing mechanism functions globally. Given that European countries tend to prioritize land transport, Japan should focus on developing maritime trade through the Black Sea. A division of labor based on naturally different perspectives and interests is essential.

Security guarantees must be multi-layered. The Ukrainian government recognizes Japan as a contributor to security guarantees at the "second" layer. This means that Japan's involvement in military affairs is limited, while other forms of assistance are highly anticipated. Ukraine seems to view Japan's participation as crucial in maintaining the economic sanctions regime. This positions Japan among countries that do not provide military support but offer other types of assistance. Unlike formal alliances such as NATO, the system of security guarantees could be envisioned as an accumulation of various types of assistance from different nations across multiple layers.

The Organization for Security and Co-operation in Europe (OSCE) is viewed unfavorably among Ukrainians due to its role in the collapse of the Minsk Agreement, for which OSCE was designated as the monitor. OSCE is unique in that both NATO members and Russia, along with other former Soviet states, are members. It is unlikely that any substantive role will be assigned to the OSCE even after the war. In theory, however, a new communication channel between Ukraine and Russia may be established. Thus, an alternative to OSCE would have to be introduced. A certain mechanism for constant communication between Ukraine and Russia ought to be created in a new ad-hoc manner, in addition to Ukraine-oriented security guarantees.

7.9 Concluding Remark

"Security guarantees" ought to be introduced upon the termination of the war. They must be designed to make a balance in the region with Russia. The contents of such concrete measures in detail will be determined in accordance with the reality at the time of negotiations. But the importance of recognizing the overall picture remains constant. The mechanism of the balance of power is required for a ceasefire to be sustained. Legitimacy needs to be considered for a peace agreement. This observation does not preclude decisions regarding when to end the war. Nevertheless, this chapter has argued that regardless of the form the termination of the war may take, the settlement must be based on a balance of power in Europe and worldwide, alongside a framework of international legitimacy.

References

Dugin, A. (2015). *Last war of the world-island: The geopolitics of contemporary Russia* (J. A. Bryant, trans).
Haushofer, K. (1931). *Geopolitik der Pan-Ideen*. Zentral-Verlag.
Herasymchuk, A., & Badrak, V. (2023). What should be the security guarantees for Ukraine? *Ukraine World*, December 19, 2023. https://ukraineworld.org/en/articles/analysis/security-guarantees-ukraine
Ikenberry, J. G. (2001). *After victory: Institutions, strategic restraint, and the rebuilding of order after major wars*. Princeton University Press.
Kissinger, H. (1994). *Diplomacy*. Simon & Schuster.
Kissinger, H. (2013). *A world restored: Metternich, Castlereagh and the problems of peace, 1812–22*. Echo Point Books & Media.
Mackinder, H. (1942). The Geographical Pivot of History, first published in 1904. In Mackinder (Ed.) *Democratic ideals and reality: A study in the politics of reconstruction*. National Defense University Press.
Mearsheimer, J. J. (2014a). Why the Ukraine crisis is the west's fault: The liberal delusions that provoked Putin. *Foreign Affairs*, 93(5).
Mearsheimer, J. J. (2014b). *Tragedy of great power politics* (updated edition). W W Norton & Co Inc.
Mearsheimer, J. J. (2022). The causes and consequences of the Ukraine war. *CSRI (Cener for International Relations and Sustain-able Development), 21* (Summer). https://www.cirsd.org/en/horizons/horizons-summer-2022-issue-no.21/the-causes-and-consequences-of-the-ukraine-war
Mills, C. (2023). Security guarantees to Ukraine. *House of Commons Library Research Briefing*, 22 July 2024. https://researchbriefings.files.parliament.uk/documents/CBP-9837/CBP-9837.pdf
President of Russia. (2021). Article by Vladimir Putin 'On the historical unity of Russians and Ukrainians', July 12, 2021. http://en.kremlin.ru/events/president/news/66181
Shinoda, H. (2000). *Re-examining Sovereignty: From classical theory to the global age*. Macmillan.
Shinoda, H. (2023). *Senso no Chiseigaku (Geopolitics of war)*. Kodansha. (in Japanese).
Shekhovtsov, A. (2008). The palingenetic thrust of Russian Neo-eurasianism: Ideas of rebirth in Aleksandr Dugin's Worldview. *Totalitarian Movements and Political Religions, 9*(4), 491–506.
Spiegel International. (2022). Interview with Henry Kissinger: 'There is no good historical example' for war in Ukraine, 15 July 2022. https://www.spiegel.de/international/world/interview-with-henry-kissinger-for-war-in-ukraine-there-is-no-good-historical-example-a-64b77d41-5b60-497e-8d2f-9041a73b1892

Tallis, B. (2023). Security guarantees for Ukraine: Until NATO membership, extending the joint expeditionary force is the best option. *German Council on Foreign Relations: Policy Brief*, Jun 30, 2023. https://dgap.org/en/research/publications/security-guarantees-ukraine-0

World Economic Forum. (2022). Kissinger: These are the main geopolitical challenges facing the world right now, May 23, 2022. https://www.weforum.org/stories/2022/05/kissinger-these-are-the-main-geopolitical-challenges-facing-the-world-right-now/

Open Access This chapter is licensed under the terms of the Creative Commons Attribution-NonCommercial-NoDerivatives 4.0 International License (http://creativecommons.org/licenses/by-nc-nd/4.0/), which permits any noncommercial use, sharing, distribution and reproduction in any medium or format, as long as you give appropriate credit to the original author(s) and the source, provide a link to the Creative Commons license and indicate if you modified the licensed material. You do not have permission under this license to share adapted material derived from this chapter or parts of it.

The images or other third party material in this chapter are included in the chapter's Creative Commons license, unless indicated otherwise in a credit line to the material. If material is not included in the chapter's Creative Commons license and your intended use is not permitted by statutory regulation or exceeds the permitted use, you will need to obtain permission directly from the copyright holder.

Chapter 8
Community Resilience in Conflict Zones: Identifying Key Factors for Conflict Resolution and Recovery Potential

Olena Akimova, Anna Ishchenko, and Iurii Perga

Contents

8.1	Introduction	102
8.2	Resilience and Local Resilience Definition	102
8.3	Resilience Factors—Literature Review	104
8.4	Historical Examples of Local Resilience in Conflict Zones	106
8.5	Methodology	108
8.6	Data Analysis	109
8.7	Gender Perspectives Integration	113
8.8	Practical Policy Recommendations	114
8.9	Conclusion	115
References		116

Abstract As the events of the Russian war in Ukraine show, the resilience of the local communities in the regions of the conflict zone and frontline regions as the ability of de-occupied communities to recover is not equal. Given the hybrid nature of modern war, its informational and manipulative component, as well as the genuine threats posed by missile and drone attacks on the territory of Ukraine, there are currently no completely safe communities. The main goal of this article is to identify the factors of local resilience and find those crucial for conflict resolution and recovery of the region. Historical examples of local resilience in conflict zones, such as the Croatian War of Independence (1991–1995), are analyzed. The construction of the Local Resilience Index is an assessment of the sustainability of different regions, focusing on different aspects such as governance efficiency, economic factors, security assessment, and social capital. The primary source for calculating the index is the data from sociological studies conducted in 2023 on representative samples in different regions of Ukraine.

Keywords Local (community) resilience · Conflict zone regions · Ukraine · Conflict resolution · Recovery potential

---

O. Akimova · A. Ishchenko (✉) · I. Perga
Igor Sikorsky Kyiv Polytechnic Institute, Kyiv, Ukraine
e-mail: a.ishchenko@kpi.ua

8.1 Introduction

The politics of any modern state is inextricably linked with the necessity of a comprehensive national security strategy. Such a policy must address a broad spectrum of threats, from conventional military threats to the increasingly prevalent cyber threats and terrorism. Moreover, modern security strategies must also account for non-traditional security challenges, including climate change, pandemics, and other global risks. A robust national security policy ensures the protection of a nation's sovereignty and fosters stability and resilience in an interconnected world where threats are multifaceted and constantly evolving. Effective national security frameworks must integrate military capabilities with diplomatic, technological, and environmental strategies, ensuring a holistic approach to safeguarding the state and its citizens. However, the effectiveness of implementing such a policy varies in different countries. In addition, public policy and administration in the field of early conflict prevention should be developed at the national, local, and regional levels. All communities develop approaches to responding to challenges, from major storms to pandemics, but some are more active in crisis preparedness and respond better to them (Levesque et al., 2024).

The particularity of Ukraine's case lies in that the question of concluding the acute phase of the war remains open. Therefore, the necessity of recovering regions affected by occupation, shelling, or hostilities, as well as strengthening communities under potential threat, is an issue that needs to be addressed simultaneously with conducting military operations to defend the country. This issue is also relevant given the global impact of the Russian war in Ukraine on the economy and security of all regions of the world without exception (for example, Dragos et al., 2023 or Mhlanga & Ndhlovu, 2023).

8.2 Resilience and Local Resilience Definition

The concept of resilience, especially in relation to hazard events, is widely applied across various fields. These include psychology and psychiatry, public health, related sciences, environmental science, engineering, and the broader spectrum of economic, social, and behavioral sciences.

Notably, most scientific research on resilience primarily focuses on the ability of local communities to withstand stresses, typically of natural origin. In our study, however, we focus on communities' capacity to resist military aggression, sustaining their critical functions and other social and socio-psychological aspects of local communities' resilience. Predominantly, factors in the latter category fall within historical, cultural, political, or religious contexts.

In the context of local resilience, we may consider several vital factors. Infrastructure resilience includes the physical structures and systems (like buildings, transportation, and utilities) essential for community functioning. Ensuring these are robust and adaptable to changes or disasters is crucial for local resilience. Social resilience involves the strength and adaptability of social networks, community organizations, and social fabric. A resilient community tends to have strong social ties, effective communication channels, and the capacity for collective action. Economic resilience pertains to the ability of a local economy to absorb shocks (such as a recession or the loss of a major employer) and to adapt to long-term changes in economic conditions. Environmental resilience involves the capacity of local ecosystems to withstand environmental changes and stresses, such as climate change or pollution, and to continue providing essential services like clean air and water. Governance and institutional resilience address effective leadership and good governance, and the presence of robust institutions is crucial for coordinating responses to challenges and implementing strategies that enhance resilience. Some studies have highlighted cyber resilience (Choi et al., 2023). Also, community resilience describes the collective ability of a neighborhood or geographically defined area to deal with stressors and efficiently resume the rhythms of daily life through cooperation following shocks (Aldrich, 2012).

Given this, we can, in some cases, rely on the interpretation of resilience through the lens of understanding the resilience of some specific sectors or critically important management objects, such as critical infrastructure. The Directive (EU) 2022/2557 (European Union, 2022) underlines resilience as a critical entity's ability to prevent, protect against, respond to, resist, mitigate, absorb, accommodate, and recover from an incident.

UNDP identifies four pillars of resilience in the war in Ukraine: crisis response, provision of public services, reconstruction for recovery and return, inclusive economic growth, and social cohesion and inclusion. These pillars are essential in addressing the challenges posed by the conflict and ensuring long-term recovery and stability for affected communities (UNDP Recovery Framework, 2024). This reflects a broader framework of understanding resilience (United Nations Development Programme, 2012) as society's ability "to smoothly respond, recover, and reconstruct when a disaster happens."

The issue of resilience is an essential component of NATO policy (Washington D.C.—4 April 1949), which actively promotes the development and support of civilian preparedness among member countries. The concept of resilience is a critical element of NATO's founding treaty, the North Atlantic Treaty (Washington, DC—April 4, 1949), which is clearly defined in Article 3. This Article commits all member states to "maintain and develop their individual and collective capacity to resist armed attack." Thus, the founding documents of NATO define the critical factors of resilience, which are mainly institutional: the continuity of government work, the provision of essential services to member countries, and the provision of civilian support to military efforts.

At the 2016 Warsaw Summit, Allied leaders committed (Commitment to enhance resilience, 2016) to improving resilience by focusing on seven key areas of civilian preparedness, including ensuring continuity of government, delivery of critical services, and resilience of energy, food, water, communications, and transportation systems. They also prioritized managing mass movements of people and responding effectively to large-scale emergencies. The pursuit of a holistic approach to understanding resilience often leads to a broader interpretation of the concept, but can sometimes result in a loss of specific context, which is crucial in the development of effective operational response plans. Nevertheless, maintaining integrity in the conceptualization of resilience is a critical step towards further operationalization. The George C. Marshall European Center for Security Studies proposes defining resilience as a comprehensive approach to regional crisis preparedness that extends beyond politico-military measures (Katsuya, 2023). This approach incorporates economic factors and emphasizes the importance of ensuring continuous access to vital goods, raw materials, and services in the face of potential escalations or crises.

Reflecting on the multi-vector nature of challenges to resilience in the face of growing hybrid threats, the Royal United Services Institute (RUSI, 2023), has called for the creation of a Center for Democratic Resilience (The Need for a Democratic Resilience Centre, 2023) to counter non-military threats, such as disinformation and cyber-attacks, that undermine trust in democratic institutions. It emphasizes the need for long-term crisis prevention measures, such as threat monitoring, sharing best practices, and developing strategies to protect democracy through international cooperation, outlining the potential of partnership and collaboration in strengthening resilience through a culture of democracy.

In turn, the theory of Norris and other scholars (Norris, 2008) presents a more interdisciplinary understanding of resilience that encompasses contemporary understandings of stress, adaptation, well-being, and resource dynamics. They viewed resilience as a process that connects resources, such as adaptive capacity, with outcomes like adaptation, preparedness, and response.

The factors identified as critical for resilience under long-term stressors, such as post-war recovery, will be different from those required during a crisis of a different nature, such as COVID-19. Similarly, the factors that influence the resilience of local communities during war and in the post-war period will differ from those that shape the resilience of an individual healthcare sector during a pandemic or the labor market in a financial crisis.

8.3 Resilience Factors—Literature Review

Resilience is generally understood as recovering from or adjusting quickly to adversity or change. It can refer to both materials and individuals. In the context of materials, resilience refers to the ability of a substance to return to its original shape after being bent, stretched, or pressed. In the context of individuals or systems, resilience often refers to the ability to withstand and recover from difficult situations. It is a dynamic process that involves coping with adversity using available resources and skills.

Local resilience in conflict zones is influenced by a range of determinants, including social, economic, environmental, and institutional factors. Research has identified the following key determinants. Strong social networks and community cohesion are often associated with higher resilience levels. As solid economic resources may give more access to livelihood opportunities, income sources, and economic diversification can enhance resilience. On the other hand, effective governance, institutions, and the rule of law are essential for building and maintaining resilience. We should also consider that the availability of essential services such as healthcare, education, and clean water contributes to community resilience.

The question of determining the factors of community resilience is also essential in the context of achieving sustainable development goals, including goal 16 on achieving sustainable peace. However, some scholars (Mhlanga & Ndhlovu, 2023) believe that current scientific papers do not pay enough attention to how war poses a risk to the achievement of SGD.

The issue of community resilience is not entirely new to research. Varghese et al. (2006) tends to show a more specific correlation between the composition of ownership and the type of local ownership and local resilience. In other words, the likelihood of setting clear objectives for supporting local employment, community initiatives, and the business's long-term sustainability increases when there is broader participation in ownership among employees, managers, and local community members.

Bulakh (2016), reflecting on the factors of resilience in eastern Ukraine, concludes that building resilience requires local ownership, capacity building, and comprehensiveness. An essential factor of resilience is the community-based approach to security and developing a sense of responsibility for community security, which can ensure a rapid response to a crisis. Anna Bulakh says that if a society can self-organize, mobilize, and provide a solid foundation for state institutions in times of crisis, a response mechanism that can define resilience is in place.

Hedenskog (2023) substantiates the idea that Ukraine's resilience after Russia's full-scale invasion on February 24, 2022, did not emerge from a vacuum. Along with reforming the armed forces and modernizing logistics, communications, and cyber defense, the author also identifies the role of civilian formal and informal activism, which has become an integral part of Ukraine's response to Russia's war.

Monika Huber's "Definition of Resilience," published by Springer Fachmedien Wiesbaden in 2023, delves into the etymology and evolution of the term 'resilience' (Huber, 2023). Initially used in material science to describe a material's ability to return to its original shape after pressure, the concept has been adapted into psychological parlance. In this context, resilience refers to navigating through and recovering from challenging life situations without enduring harm. This definition implies that resilience manifests in response to adversity, relying on existing resources and skills, and is not an inherent trait.

Huber's work further explores resilience as a domain-specific attribute, acquired through experiences and only partially transferable across different life areas. This perspective frames resilience as a dynamic and active process, emphasizing the role of active adaptation in the face of adversity. Central to this concept is the maintenance or rapid restoration of mental health during and after challenging situations, highlighting resilience's active and process-oriented nature.

Additionally, Huber emphasizes that resilience is not solely a crisis management tool but also a crucial element in natural developmental processes. It fosters self-efficacy, confidence in one's abilities and resources, and the belief in overcoming obstacles to achieve specific goals. This broader view of resilience underscores its significance in overcoming adversity and promoting personal growth and development.

In "Cities in a Time of Terror: Space, Territory, and Local Resilience" by Savitch (2015), the concept of urban terrorism is explored as a strategy that exploits a city's inherent strengths to induce self-implosion. Savitch identifies three fundamental logics guiding terrorist targeting of urban areas. The author emphasizes local resilience, conceptualized as a city's ability to recover from terrorist attacks. Additionally, it offers insights into sustaining and enhancing this resilience, providing a comprehensive analysis of urban terrorism and its implications for city planning and security.

Mamediieva and Moynihan (2023) consider the potential of digital government and analyze how the war was the impetus for the acceleration of the use of digital capabilities, which were used not only for defensive military purposes but also to ensure the continuity of civilian aspects of public administration, in particular the provision of digital documentation and assistance to displaced persons. According to the authors' conclusions, digital capabilities have become a fundamental basis for Ukraine's resilience.

Considering that rebuilding and ensuring community stability in Ukraine remains urgent even amidst ongoing warfare, the approach proposed by Olsson and Moore offers valuable insights (Olsson & Moore, 2024). They suggest that the transition from a state of war or violent conflict necessitates a fundamental transformation. However, it is crucial to note that such transformations do not inherently guarantee peace, stability, or justice; these outcomes require deliberate and sustained efforts. The authors focus on the transient phase, when the system is in a suspended state between the existing dominant state and a new alternative state. Developing a theoretical framework for understanding peacebuilding as a transformative process of change, the authors of the study advocate combining resilience-based transformations and transformative justice research to address the complex dynamics of peacebuilding, given that peacebuilding processes are a form of crisis-induced transformation.

8.4 Historical Examples of Local Resilience in Conflict Zones

The resilience of Croatia during *the Croatian War of Independence (1991–1995)* offers a notable example of local resilience in a conflict zone. This conflict, part of the broader Yugoslav Wars, was characterized by intense and widespread fighting and significant political and ethnic tensions.

Despite the challenges of war, Croatian communities often displayed remarkable cohesion and solidarity. Local initiatives to support displaced persons, organize humanitarian aid, and provide medical services were critical in sustaining the civilian population during the conflict.

They are faced with aggression, Croatian forces and local militias organized effective defensive strategies. Notable examples include the defense of Vukovar and other besieged towns, where, despite being heavily outnumbered and outgunned, local defenders held out for extended periods against Yugoslav and Serb forces, demonstrating resilience and determination.

The Croatian economy faced significant disruptions due to the war. However, there was a concerted effort to adapt to the wartime economy, with production and trade patterns shifting to support the war effort and sustain the population.

Throughout the conflict, there was a strong emphasis on maintaining Croatian cultural identity and heritage. This was seen in efforts to protect historical sites and cultural artifacts from destruction and in the continuation of cultural and religious practices under challenging circumstances.

Croatia's efforts to gain international recognition and support were crucial to its resilience. The recognition of Croatia's independence by the European Community and other nations in January 1992 helped legitimize its position and enabled access to international support and diplomatic channels.

Following the end of hostilities, Croatia faced the challenge of rebuilding and reintegrating war-affected areas. Efforts in reconstruction, reconciliation, and the return of displaced persons were crucial aspects of Croatia's post-conflict resilience.

We can defy familiar and different aspects of local resilience between the Croatian case in 1991–1995 and the Ukrainian case in 2022–2023. In Croatia and Ukraine, strong community solidarity and cohesion have been critical in facing the challenges of war. Local initiatives, volunteer efforts, and support networks have played vital roles in providing humanitarian aid, medical care, and support for displaced persons.

Both countries have shown remarkable resilience in organizing their defense against aggression. This includes mobilizing and training military forces, developing local militias or territorial defense units, and employing strategic defensive tactics suited to their respective terrains and situations.

Both Croatia and Ukraine have actively sought international support and recognition. Diplomatic efforts to garner political, economic, and military assistance have been crucial in sustaining their resilience in conflict.

The economies of both countries had to adapt to wartime conditions, with shifts in production, trade, and resource allocation. Economic resilience has been vital to maintaining normalcy and supporting the war effort.

On the other hand, the international legal and political contexts differ significantly between the two conflicts. The Croatian War occurred during the dissolution of Yugoslavia and amid a broader redefinition of national borders in Eastern Europe. On the other hand, the Ukraine conflict involves territorial integrity and sovereignty issues under the current international legal framework, including the UN Charter and various international treaties. Croatia's conflict was part of the early post-Cold War era, whereas Ukraine's conflict occurred in a more established post-Cold War international order. This impacts the nature of international alliances, geopolitical strategies, and the involvement of major powers.

One of the most significant differences is the extensive use of digital communication and social media in the Ukrainian conflict. Platforms like Twitter, Facebook, and Telegram have been crucial for real-time information sharing, humanitarian aid coordination, support mobilization, and narrative dissemination. In contrast, such platforms did not exist during the Croatian War, and information dissemination relied more on traditional media like television, radio, and newspapers. In Ukraine, technology is also used to bolster civilian resilience. Mobile apps for early warning of air raids, online platforms for coordinating volunteer efforts, and crowdfunding for humanitarian and military support are examples of how technology empowers civilians in conflict zones. Such tools were unavailable during the Croatian War, where resilience efforts relied more on physical networks and traditional forms of communication.

8.5 Methodology

Developing the Local Resilience Index aims to assess different regions' capacity to withstand and recover from crises by analyzing key dimensions such as governance efficiency, economic stability, security conditions, and the robustness of social capital. This framework offers a comprehensive evaluation of regional resilience across these critical factors, providing valuable insights into the strengths and vulnerabilities that may influence a region's ability to navigate and emerge stronger from crises (Table 8.1).

The Local Resilience Index primarily draws on data from sociological surveys conducted in 2023, which utilized representative samples from various regions of Ukraine. This methodology was chosen for two key reasons: firstly, to ensure the reliability and accuracy of the regional data, and secondly, to capture the diverse socio-economic and governance conditions across the country, enabling a more

Table 8.1 Division of regions of Ukraine into macro-regions

Administrative units of Ukraine	Macro-regions
Kyiv	Kyiv (capital city)
Zhytomyr, Kyiv, Sumy, Chernihiv Regions	North
Volyn, Rivne, Lviv, Ivano-Frankivsk, Ternopil, Zakarpattia, Chernivtsi Regions	West
Vinnytsia, Dnipropetrovsk, Kirovohrad, Poltava, Cherkasy, Khmelnytsky Regions	Center
Zaporizhzhia, Mykolaiv, Odesa, Kherson Regions	South
Donetsk, Luhansk, Kharkiv Regions	East

nuanced assessment of resilience. Sociological data offer the flexibility and promptness required for studying shifts in public consciousness compared to state statistical data, which typically exhibit significant time lags. Moreover, objective circumstances hinder access to a substantial portion of state statistical data and reports from government bodies. These are due to legal conditions imposed by the martial law in Ukraine, which restrict the disclosure of certain types of official government data. However, some of the data was collected from state statistical sources, as, in our opinion, it could not be adequately replaced by alternative indicators. This includes data on the Gross Regional Product of Ukrainian regions (as of 2021) and information regarding the housing stock condition prior to the large-scale invasion. Moreover, this study utilizes data from analytical reports (Eastern Europe Foundation 2023), statistical datasets (Ministry of Youth and Sports of Ukraine 2022, 2023; State Statistics Service of Ukraine 2023), and the results of sociological research (Info Sapiens 2023; Kyiv International Institute of Sociology 2023).

The index considers a multitude of factors across different domains:

Governance Effectiveness: Evaluating how effectively local governments can respond to and manage crises.
Economic Factors: Assessing the impact of the crisis on property damage, employment status, and other economic indicators.
Social Capital: Measuring aspects like population migration patterns, community cohesion, and public trust in institutions.
Security Aspects: Measuring aspects like the region's criminogenic situation, self-evaluation of the population's psychological exhaustion, and safety needs (Table 8.2).

8.6 Data Analysis

Index exploration provides a comparative analysis of local resilience indicators across different regions of Ukraine, delineated by specific metrics. The Index illustrates that Kyiv and the Western and Central regions possess relatively higher resilience across all categories, whereas the Eastern region demonstrates the lowest levels of resilience (Fig. 8.1).

The indicators of the western, central, and Kyiv regions have distinct characteristics. For example, Kyiv exhibits the highest Economic Potential Indicator at 0.86, a substantial Social Capital Indicator at 0.48, a robust Security Indicator at 0.63, and a relatively lower institutional one at 0.36. Specifically, Kyiv exhibits the highest economic potential in the sample, maintaining its role as the country's business and administrative hub. Even though Kyiv has been one of the most vulnerable regions since the onset of the invasion, targeted by significant resources and efforts of the aggressor, and as of 2024, continues to be subjected to regular, intense aerial bombardments, the capital has demonstrated high resilience indicators. It should be noted that some enterprises relocated their offices at the beginning of the invasion,

Table 8.2 Indicators and datasets forming the local resilience index

Aspect	Indicator, data
Governance effectiveness	Reconstruction Efficiency Indicator (Population's Expectation Alignment with Reconstruction Status): Measures the level to which the state of reconstruction meets the population's expectations NGO Interaction Indicator (Assessment of Potential for Partnership Creation Between Local Authorities and Your Organization): Evaluates the potential for establishing partnerships between local government bodies and organizations Overall Government Effectiveness Indicator (Proportion of Population Deeming the Actions of Ukrainian Authorities Effective Since the Start of the Russo-Ukraine War): Assesses the public perception of the effectiveness of government actions since the onset of the conflict Trust in Local Government Level: Indicates the degree of public trust in local governing bodies
Economic factors	Criticality Indicator of Civil Infrastructure Destruction (Proportion of Population with Property Damage): Measures the extent of damage to civilian infrastructure experienced by the population Population Welfare Indicator: Proportion of Population Demonstrating a Need for Financial Assistance: Assesses the population segment indicating a need for monetary support Unemployment Rate: Measures the proportion of the labor force without a job Gross Regional Product in Current Prices, Million UAH, for 2020): Reflects the total economic output of a region in the specified year Housing Need Indicator (Proportion of Population Living in Temporary Accommodations): Evaluates the percentage of individuals residing in temporary housing, such as hotels, dormitories, or with friends, relatives, or other unfamiliar persons Reconstruction Needs Indicator (Ratio of Emergency Housing Area per Capita): Assesses the extent of housing in disrepair relative to the population size
Social capital factors	Reintegration Indicator (Proportion of Those Who Left Their Homes and Later Returned): Measures the percentage of individuals who had to leave their homes but subsequently returned Settlement Indicator (Proportion of Those Who Stayed in Their Homes): Indicates the percentage of the population that remained in their homes during the conflict Settlement Indicator (Conflict Resilience - Proportion of Those Who Do Not Plan to Leave Their Homes in Case of Conflict Escalation): Assesses the resilience of individuals in conflict situations, precisely their intention to stay in their homes despite conflict escalation Religiosity Indicator (Proportion of the Population Expressing Trust in the Church): Measures the population segment indicating trust in religious institutions Social Distance Indicator (Proportion of the Population Trusting No One): Evaluates the level of mistrust or social distancing within the population

(continued)

Table 8.2 (continued)

Aspect	Indicator, data
Security aspect	Housing Need Indicator (Proportion of Those in Greatest Need of Safe Housing): Assesses the population segment with an urgent need for secure living conditions Safety Need Indicator (Proportion of Those Who Do Not Feel Safe): Measures the percentage of individuals who do not feel safe in their current environment Psychological Exhaustion Indicator (Proportion of Those Willing to Receive Psychological Assistance): Evaluates the percentage of the population indicating a readiness to receive psychological support Criminogenic Indicator (Ratio of the Number of People Who Died Due to Criminal Offenses to the Total Population): This metric evaluates the proportion of individuals who have died due to criminal activities and the overall population size

Index Calculation Steps included normalizing the data, assigning weights to different factors, and aggregating these to form an overall resilience score for each region

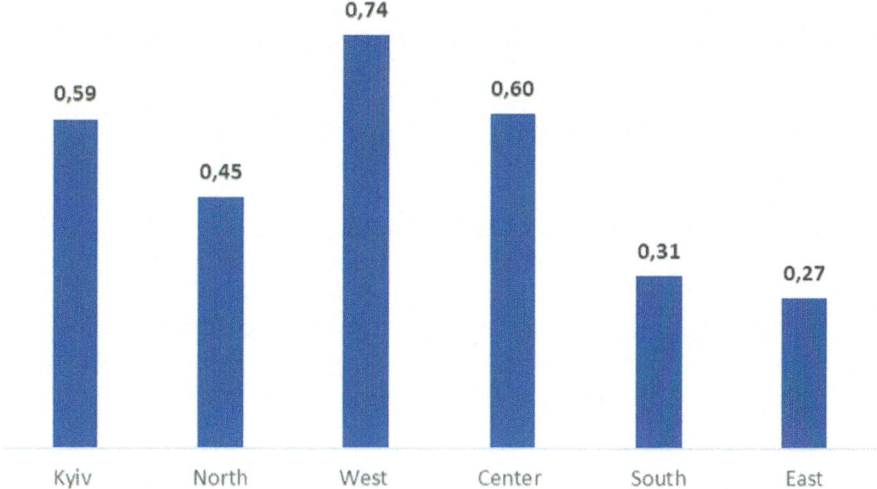

Fig. 8.1 Local resilience index (regional dimension)

which posed a threat to Kyiv's status as a business center. According to expert calculations (Mixfin, 2024), as of November 2023, nearly 7820 Ukrainian companies have relocated since the end of February 2022. Almost one-third of the relocated enterprises (27%, totaling 2111 businesses) moved from Kyiv. However, the resilience of the state governance system (the state authorities did not relocate their offices even at the start of the invasion), coupled with the effective strengthening of the city's defense systems, have created conditions under which Kyiv currently shows the highest resilience index scores.

The Western region of Ukraine exhibits high resilience indicators for somewhat different reasons. Primarily, this region is home to areas perceived as the safest in the country, being the most distant from the eastern border and out of reach for certain types of weaponry as of January 2024. However, this does not mean the region suffered negligible losses due to the invasion. Initially, it received unprecedented numbers of internally displaced people, with evacuation trains arriving from eastern, central, and southern regions. Many displaced individuals continued to Western European countries, but many remained in the region. Furthermore, the Western region has become a hub for business relocation. Additionally, it shows high social capital indicators, which traditionally have robust social and cultural mechanisms for reinforcement. This region records the highest levels of social cohesion (high trust in the church, low social distance indicators). It is least affected by outgoing migration processes, as it has the highest proportion of people who do not plan to leave their residence in the event of conflict escalation and the most significant number of people who have never left their homes. Despite high safety indicators, the region is not a leader in the reintegration indicator, i.e., the proportion of people who have returned home after migration (Fig. 8.2).

The Central region of Ukraine is characterized as the most balanced in terms of various indicators. This region uniformly displays relatively high safety indicators, social-institutional potential, and economic resources. However, it exhibits a somewhat underdeveloped component of social capital. Notably, this indicator is inherently inert and not susceptible to rapid managerial influences, as the conditions for its enhancement are formed over generations. Nevertheless, from a recovery perspective, this region can be considered favorable. It is noteworthy for its balanced social distance indicators, which provide a conducive base for initiating recovery projects, further strengthened by the considerable trust of the population in the government (due to approval of the government's actions since the beginning of the invasion) and an adequate level of trust in local authorities. Among the risks for this region are critical economic well-being indicators and challenges in housing infrastructure recovery, which inevitably exert pressure on social tension indicators, potentially diminishing public trust in the governing system and weakening its capacity for recovery project implementation.

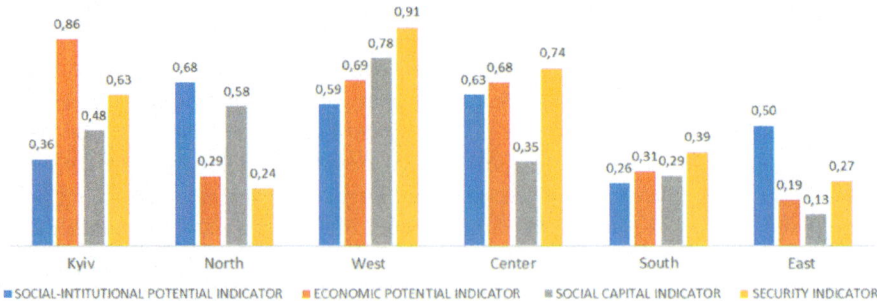

Fig. 8.2 Local resilience indicators

The Northern region is identified as the most unbalanced in terms of the selected indicators, yet it exhibits strong positions in specific categories. Notably, the region is characterized by high social-institutional potential and social capital. These factors create favorable conditions for implementing recovery projects that rely on the interaction between the authorities and the community. In the Northern region, we observe one of the highest potentials for creating partnerships between local authorities and NGOs, a high level of government effectiveness as assessed by the local population, and the best indicator for meeting expectations in ongoing reconstruction projects. This is evidenced by one of the highest reintegration rates of the population that left their homes. Notably, the region has the highest indicator of social cohesion in terms of trust level.

At the same time, it is essential to note that this region faces significant economic risks. The local authorities are under additional pressure due to high unemployment levels, high rates of financial need among the population, and an unfavorable criminogenic situation, consequently leading to high levels of psychological exhaustion among the residents.

As for psychological stability, the following conclusions were made in the study of the volunteer community (Pidbutska et al., 2023) regarding the need for specially organized psychological help and support. The constant danger of activity, the need to be in contact with different people, and moral fatigue lead to rapid emotional exhaustion and can cause health disorders or even cost one's life.

The Southern and Eastern regions are understandably the most vulnerable regarding recovery. These areas face the most acute social and economic challenges due to their prolonged proximity to active conflict zones. They suffer the most significant infrastructural damage, and their populations are in the most precarious position regarding safety. This situation exemplifies the cumulative effects of the war, most prominently observed in these regions. They require the most extensive efforts and resources for recovery.

8.7 Gender Perspectives Integration

In conflict resilience and recovery, integrating gender perspectives ensures an inclusive and balanced approach to community rebuilding. Conflicts often disproportionately affect women and other marginalized gender groups, making it essential to address their specific needs in resilience-building efforts. Policies and programs should focus on gender-sensitive approaches that ensure equal participation in decision-making processes and access to recovery resources.

For example, creating leadership programs to empower women to take active roles in local governance and resilience-building initiatives can enhance the overall effectiveness of recovery. Women's networks and organizations can be key actors in promoting social cohesion, peacebuilding, and economic recovery, particularly in post-conflict contexts. Additionally, addressing gender-based violence (GBV), which often increases in conflict zones, should be a central element of any resilience strategy. Providing safe spaces, healthcare, and legal support for victims of GBV, alongside mental health services, will contribute to both immediate recovery and long-term stability.

Gender mainstreaming in infrastructure rebuilding is also essential. The design and reconstruction of public spaces should account for the specific needs of women and other vulnerable groups, ensuring accessibility and safety. For instance, rebuilding projects should include considerations for women's safety, such as adequate lighting, safe transportation options, and access to sanitation facilities, especially in temporary housing and shelters.

By integrating gender perspectives into resilience-building policies, regions will promote equality and tap into the unique contributions that women and other gender groups bring to peacebuilding and recovery processes. This approach ensures a more comprehensive and sustainable recovery where all community members participate actively.

8.8 Practical Policy Recommendations

Based on the findings and the comparative analysis of resilience in different conflict zones, several actionable policy recommendations can be made to enhance local resilience in Ukraine and other regions affected by conflict. First, strengthening local governance is essential for coordinating efforts between civil society, NGOs, and international organizations. Local governments should establish dedicated departments or task forces focused on resilience-building, ensuring continuous communication and collaboration with relevant stakeholders. This framework would streamline efforts and enhance the ability to respond effectively to crises.

Second, developing social capital through community-based initiatives should be prioritized. Programs promoting volunteerism and building trust between residents and local authorities are crucial. Fostering solid social ties through workshops on conflict resolution and facilitating dialogues among diverse community groups can strengthen long-term social cohesion and resilience. Such initiatives will enable communities to better withstand and recover from the impacts of conflict.

Third, targeted programs must support economic recovery, particularly for small businesses. Microgrants or micro-finance schemes should be implemented to help businesses rebuild in regions with high unemployment and economic disruption. These initiatives would empower local economies and create sustainable livelihoods for residents returning to their homes.

Fourth, infrastructure rebuilding should focus on immediate and long-term resilience. Critical civil infrastructure, including roads, schools, and hospitals, must be rebuilt using modern resilience principles for potential future conflicts or disasters. This approach will ensure that infrastructure is more durable and capable of withstanding future shocks.

Finally, providing robust psychological and health support is vital, particularly for volunteers and residents who have endured prolonged conflict. Establishing accessible psychological aid stations, coupled with community mental health education programs, will address trauma and stress caused by the war. These support systems are essential for fostering long-term recovery and rebuilding the psychological resilience of war-affected populations.

8.9 Conclusion

Several key insights can be derived by drawing on historical examples of community resilience during armed conflicts and incorporating the findings from the resilience indexing of Ukrainian regions. These insights are instrumental in identifying the most effective management strategies and policy decisions that can enhance regional recovery and bolster resilience in the face of wartime challenges. By leveraging these generalizations, decision-makers can better tailor their approaches to support regions in overcoming adversity and promoting long-term stability.

The developed Index highlights four core dimensions of community resilience: Governance Effectiveness, Economic Factors, Social Capital, and Security. Conclusions and recommendations for these aspects, defining community resilience, can be summarized as follows.

The crucial role of the social-institutional factor in community resilience can be reinforced through strengthening local governance and personal leadership. Examples of personal leadership by community leaders (such as Vitaliy Kim, head of the Mykolaiv Regional State Administration) allow us to discuss the impact of competent leadership on coordinating rehabilitation efforts during the war, their effectiveness, and their relevance. At the level of small and medium-sized communities, local leadership and management should be supported by professional development programs and strengthening human resources in areas related to conflict resolution, critical thinking development, and other essential soft and hard skills during complex security situations. Undoubtedly, the role of education cannot be overemphasized, even at the level of average citizens. The dissemination of knowledge on providing first aid and dealing with injuries is essential. The basics of survival and self-defense should be included in formal and informal education institutions and adapted for individuals of different ages. Additionally, developing programs and initiatives to support gender equality contributes to faster and more balanced community recovery. Communities with strong social networks and active civic engagement demonstrate higher resilience. Strengthening local organizations and fostering cooperation between citizens and local authorities are essential for building trust and cohesion.

Social and humanitarian aid programs can promote the development of social capital factors. Developing programs to improve living conditions and social infrastructure is crucial in community recovery. It is essential to build institutional capacity in healthcare within the community. Regardless of the distance of communities from conflict zones, even the most remote communities need the deployment of rehabilitation facilities (including war veterans), the implementation of a system of psychosocial support, and psychological assistance.

It should be noted that this research was dedicated to examining community resilience factors using the case of Ukraine, which is already affected by war. However, developing a community resilience index is relevant for countries currently at war and those not directly in a state of war. Such an index can serve as a basis for developing a conflict prevention system, tracking the dynamics of indicators, and developing management tools aimed primarily at preventing conflicts rather than minimizing their harmful impact.

Acknowledgements In preparing this work, we utilized technical tools, specifically ChatGPT-4o and Grammarly, solely to enhance the clarity and style of written language. These tools were employed to refine language expression without altering the substance or originality of the content.

References

Aldrich, D. P. (2012). *Building resilience: Social capital in post-disaster recovery*. University of Chicago Press.

Bulakh, A. (2016, December 22). Defining Ukraine's national resilience in light of non-linear threats: Where to start? *Commentary*. https://icds.ee/en/defining-ukraines-national-resilience-in-light-of-non-linear-threats-where-to-start/

Choi, S.-H., Youn, J., Kim, K., Lee, S., Kwon, O.-J., & Shin, D. (2023). Cyber-resilience evaluation methods focusing on response time to cyber infringement. *Sustainability, 15*(18), 13404. https://doi.org/10.3390/su151813404

Dragos, D., Dinca, C., Nicolescu, C. E., & Dogaru Cruceanu, T. (2023). The impact of the Ukrainian war on the resilience and sustainability of the local public administration in Romania: An exploratory study. *Romanian Journal of European Affairs, 23*, 64.

Eastern Europe Foundation. (2023, October). *Study of the Ukrainian civil society sector in a time of war*. Eastern Europe Foundation. http://surl.li/ppnmz

Hedenskog, J. (2023, April). Explaining Ukrainian resilience. *SCEEUS Report Series on Ukrainian Domestic Affairs, No. 2*. https://sceeus.se/en/publications/explaining-ukrainian-resilience/

Huber, M. (2023). Definition of resilience. *Springer Fachmedien Wiesbaden*. https://doi.org/10.1007/978-3-658-39782-1_3

Info Sapiens. (2023). The needs and views of Ukrainian citizens on how the post-war reconstruction of Ukraine should be carried out: Presentation of the public opinion research. *Info Sapiens*. https://www.sapiens.com.ua/publications/socpol-research/298/Wave2_final_public.pdf

Katsuya, M. (2023). *Resilience and reciprocity: The future of partnership amidst strategic simultaneity*. Retrieved October 29, 2024, from https://www.marshallcenter.org/sites/default/files/files/2023-08/Security%20Insights%2077_Katsuya_Resilience%20and%20Reciprocity.pdf

Kyiv International Institute of Sociology. (2023, October 31). Dynamics of perception of the direction of affairs in Ukraine and trust in certain institutions between May 2022 and October 2023. *Kyiv International Institute of Sociology*. http://surl.li/ppnmd

Levesque, V. R., Bell, K. P., & Johnson, E. S. (2024). The role of municipal digital services in advancing rural resilience. *Government Information Quarterly, 41*(1). https://doi.org/10.1016/j.giq.2023.101883

Mamediieva, G., & Moynihan, D. (2023). Digital resilience in wartime: The case of Ukraine. *Public Administration Review*. https://doi.org/10.1111/puar.13742

Mhlanga, D., & Ndhlovu, E. (2023). The implications of the Russia–Ukraine war on sustainable development goals in Africa. *Fudan Journal of the Humanities and Social Sciences*. https://doi.org/10.1007/s40647-023-00383-z

Ministry of Youth and Sports of Ukraine. (2022). Migration and socio-political attitudes. *Ministry of Youth and Sports of Ukraine*. http://surl.li/ppnmb

Ministry of Youth and Sports of Ukraine. (2023). The impact of war on youth in Ukraine. *Ministry of Youth and Sports of Ukraine*. http://surl.li/jddbi

Mixfin. (2024, January 4). Relocation of Ukrainian business: Opendatabot statistics. *Mixfin*. https://mixfin.com/ua/blog/relokatsiia-biznesu-v-ukraini

Olsson, P., & Moore, M.-L. (2024). A resilience-based transformations approach to peacebuilding and transformative justice. *Current Opinion in Environmental Sustainability, 66*, 101392. https://doi.org/10.1016/j.cosust.2023.101392

Pidbutska, N., Knysh, A., & Demidova, Y. (2023). Psychological safety of volunteers during the war. *Journal of Education Culture and Society, 14*(1), 66–75. https://doi.org/10.15503/jecs2023.1.66.75

RUSI. (2023). The need for a democratic resilience centre. *Royal United Services Institute*. https://rusi.org/explore-our-research/publications/commentary/need-for-democratic-resilience-centre

Savitch, H. V. (2015). *Cities in a time of terror: Space, territory, and local resilience*. Routledge. https://doi.org/10.4324/9781315705675

State Statistics Service of Ukraine. (2023). Statistical collection of the regions of Ukraine, book 1. *State Statistics Service of Ukraine*. http://surl.li/ppnmh

Varghese, J., Krogman, N. T., Beckley, T. M., & Nadeau, S. (2006). Critical analysis of the relationship between local ownership and community resiliency. *Environmental Management, 71*(3), 505–527. https://doi.org/10.1526/003601106778070653

UNDP Recovery Framework for Ukraine (United Nations Development Programme in Ukraine). (2024). https://www.undp.org/ukraine/publications/undp-recovery-framework-ukraine

United Nations Development Programme. (2012). Recovery resilient and prevention in investing development of heart the at resilience. *UNDP*. https://www.undp.org/sites/g/files/zskgke326/files/publications/1206_undp_en_out%20(%20in%20English).pdf

Open Access This chapter is licensed under the terms of the Creative Commons Attribution-NonCommercial-NoDerivatives 4.0 International License (http://creativecommons.org/licenses/by-nc-nd/4.0/), which permits any noncommercial use, sharing, distribution and reproduction in any medium or format, as long as you give appropriate credit to the original author(s) and the source, provide a link to the Creative Commons license and indicate if you modified the licensed material. You do not have permission under this license to share adapted material derived from this chapter or parts of it.

The images or other third party material in this chapter are included in the chapter's Creative Commons license, unless indicated otherwise in a credit line to the material. If material is not included in the chapter's Creative Commons license and your intended use is not permitted by statutory regulation or exceeds the permitted use, you will need to obtain permission directly from the copyright holder.

Conclusion: The Russo–Ukrainian War and Global Order Melting into the Air?

The book offers various insights into the impacts of the Russo–Ukrainian War. The authors do not claim to provide a comprehensive picture of the war's impacts. Rather, this work aims to draw attention to some of the key issues related to the conflict. The authors hope these efforts will help broaden perspectives and stimulate thought about the war.

The book began by examining fundamental questions about names, concepts, and theories of war, with a particular focus on the Russo–Ukrainian War. The authors also described the war's impact on international politics and Ukrainian society, with special attention to the relationship between NATO and Ukraine. This volume further explored the resilience of local communities in Ukraine and considers the implications of mediation, conflict resolution, geopolitics, and international relations theories for Ukraine's future.

As we compiled this book, the war continued, with no clear prospect for its resolution. This can be a frustrating endeavor, as the book itself may not directly influence events on the battlefield. Nevertheless, the authors believe that efforts to understand the war's effects in depth will help pave the way toward constructive steps forward. Regardless of the way the war ends, the people of Ukraine will need to find a path to rebuild their society, and the international community, including Japan, should be better prepared to assist them. The authors recognize the need to continue elaborating on key issues and addressing policy agendas more concretely. For now, they hope this book represents one step in envisioning a future beyond the conflict.

This book revolves around Ukraine and is for Ukraine. Yet it certainly goes beyond a single nation's concerns given the magnitude and consequential nature of the Russo–Ukrainian War. After all, geography matters. We have a war in the geographical center of Europe where the mightiest nuclear power (Russia) has attacked the biggest European nation (Ukraine). Both countries have a dilapidated yet still powerful industrial base. We have also bear in mind that this Russian war against Ukraine predates the full-scale invasion of February 2022. Russian armed incursions had begun with a seizure of Crimea and occupation of parts of Eastern Ukraine in 2014. It is not for no reason that Zbigniew Brzezinski—an influential American political scientist and the US National Security Advisor to President Jimmy Carter—repeatedly expressed his dictum that without Ukraine no restoration of Russian imperialist powers would be possible, therefore Russian control over Ukraine would be an indispensable element of its project of imperial resurgence (Brzezinski, 1997). The Russian aggression against Ukraine is a testimony to his prediction. The Russia instigated the Russo–Ukrainian War is a direct affront to the rule based global system.

U.S. Defence Secretary in Biden's administration Loyd Austin III in his Foreign Affairs piece opined forcefully and eloquently on the implications of the Russian invasion of Ukraine: "Putin's assault is a warning. It is a sneak preview of a world built by tyrants and thugs—a chaotic, violent world carved into spheres of influence; a world where bullies trample their smaller neighbors; and a world where aggressors force free people to live in fear. So we face a hinge in history" (Austin, 2024).

Illustrious British historian Eric Hobsbawm who witnessed such tragic and tectonic moments of history as the rise of fascism, World War I, Holocaust, the Cold War, and the Leninist extinction (to borrow UC Berkeley political science Ken Jowitt terminology) titled his autobiography "Interesting Times" (Hobsbawm, 2003; Jowitt, 1992). It was a reflection of a historian's idiosyncratic and perhaps self-ironic attitude towards the world when tumulus periods in the dynamics of human societies are deemed interesting. We are also living through interesting times. The Russian war against Ukraine may be a sound of a death knell for existing—imperfect as it may be—global order. Replacement of some sort of order with a Hobbesian war of all against all.

Since we are discussing actions of states it is legitimate to encode the language of geopolitics. Return of geopolitical rivalries will bring about only one thing for human societies—they will become increasingly drawn into various conflicts or, to apply Hobbes's famous quote, the life of such states will become solitary, poor, nasty, brutish, and short (Hobbes, 1914: XIX). After the contributors of the book were finished with writing their chapters, two major news came in. Donald Trump staged a dramatic comeback to the White House and it was reputed that Ukrainian Armed Forces clashed with North Korean troops fighting on a Russian side. The world's propensity to live dangerously has dramatically increased. The founder of the world-systems analysis American sociologist Immanuel Wallerstein prophesized in the 1990s about the end of the world as we know it (Wallerstein, 1999). Back then his vision appeared to be excessively grim. Now it seems to be a self-fulfilling prophecy.

It is a pundit's job to supply the public, politicians and policy-makers with a reliable account of what's happening in the world, how to interpret it and what is perhaps the most important part—how to deal with it.

Finally, the authors with sadness and admiration dedicate this book to all those who have been killed as a result of the Russian war on Ukraine and those who have courageously sacrificed their lives for Ukraine's freedom.

References

Austin III, L. J. (2024). The price of principle is dwarfed by the cost of capitulation in Ukraine: What's at stake in Kyiv's fight for freedom. *Foreign Affairs*, November 1, 2024. https://www.foreignaffairs.com/ukraine/price-principle-dwarfed-cost-capitulation-ukraine. Accessed on November 6, 2024.
Brzezinski, Z. (1997). *The grand chessboard: American primacy and its geostrategic imperatives*. Basic Books.
Hobbes, T. (1914). *The Leviathan*. Dent Publishers.
Hobsbawm, E. (2003). *Interesting times: A twentieth-century life*. Pantheon.
Jowitt, K. (1992). *The new world disorder: The Leninist extinction*. University of California Press.
Wallerstein, I. (1999). *The end of the world as we know it: Social science for the twenty-first century*. University of Minnesota Press.

The manufacturer's authorised representative in the EU is Springer Nature Customer Service Centre GmbH, Europaplatz 3, 69115 Heidelberg, Germany. If you have any concerns regarding our products, please contact ProductSafety@springernature.com

Printed and bound by CPI Group (UK) Ltd, Croydon, CR0 4YY
26/03/2026
02078940-0012